ENVIRONMENT
AND OUR GLOBAL COMMUNITY

CR£O

Susan G. Shapiro, editor

international debate education association
New York • Amsterdam • Brussels

Published by

international debate education association

400 West 59th Street / New York, NY 10019

Copyright © 2005 by Open Society Institute

Activity sheets may be downloaded from www.idebate.org/environment.htm.

You can reach Susan Shapiro through her web site at www.thecurtainrises.com.

Library of Congress Cataloging-in-Publication Data

Environment and our global community / Susan G. Shapiro, editor.
       p. cm.
ISBN 1-932716-12-2
ISBN 978-1-932716-12-2
   1. Environmental education--Activity programs. 2. Environmental
  education--Curricula. 3. Environmental responsibility--Study and
  teaching (Elementary)--Activity programs.   I. Shapiro, Susan,
  1947-   .
  GE77.E58 2006
  333.7--dc22

                                                    2005021720

Design by Hernan Bonomo
Printed in the USA

 IDEBATE Press

ACKNOWLEDGMENTS

The publication of this curriculum was made possible through the collaborative efforts of environmental and education experts in 18 different countries. The immense task of coordinating the minute details of this information was made possible by the tireless efforts of Susan Shapiro (project director), Lisa Pilsitz (editor), and Joyce Libal (environmental consultant), with the support of Carol Flaherty-Zonis (associate project director).

In addition we would like to acknowledge the coordinators of the Open Society Institute's Health Education Network Program in each of the countries that participated in the writing of the curriculum. In the true spirit of the program these coordinators found some of the best environmental education specialists in their countries to contribute to this international effort.

The Open Society Institute would like to give special acknowledgment to the Central and Eastern European environmental experts who contributed material for specific chapters in the curriculum. A list of the contributing experts and the chapters they contributed follows.

Elizabeth Lorant
Sarah Klaus
Open Society Institute

CONTRIBUTING AUTHORS

Sirje Aher (Estonia)

Simona Botea (Romania)

Sanja Derviskadic-Jovanovic (Bosnia)

Aco Divac (Yugoslavia)

Nataly Dobrotina (Russia)

Dr. Bohdan Dudek (Poland)

Laima Galkute (Lithuania)

Tatiana Gryaznova (Russia)

Agnes Halacsy (Hungary)

Jorg Hodalic (Slovenia)

Dorottya Hollo (Hungary)

Vera Janikova (Czech Republic)

Bozica Jelusic (Croatia)

Oksana Kiseleva (Moldova)

Dorota Merecz (Poland)

Boris Isaakovich Moutchnick (Russia)

Lidija Pavic (Croatia)

Natalia Pustovit (Ukraine)

Sulejman Redzic (Bosnia)

Sergej Shustov (Russia)

Irine Shwetz (Russia)

Stefan Szabo (Slovak Republic)

Silvia Szabova (Slovak Republic)

Maria Szlka (Hungary)

Josif Tanevski (Macedonia)

Virginia Valova (Bulgaria)

Irena Vangjeli (Albania)

Rata Vocisa (Latvia)

The Open Society Institute would also like to acknowledge its Health Education Network Program Coordinators for their assistance in the development of this curriculum: Valdeta Sala (Albania); Svetlana Zec and Hazim Kazic (Bosnia); Virginia Valova and Roumen Valchev (Bulgaria); Darko Tot (Croatia); Vera Janikova (Czech Republic); Mare Kraav (Estonia); Eva Foldvari (Hungary); Solvita Lazdina (Latvia); Zina Baltreniene (Lithuania); Ratka Kuljan (Macedonia); Julia Moldoveanu (Moldova); Grazyna Budzinska (Poland); Dan Baciu (Romania); Steve de Bethune (Russia); Tatiana Gryaznova (Russia); Tatiana Melnikova (Russia); Jana Hazirova (Slovakia); Brankica Petkovic (Slovenia); Olena Sichkar (Ukraine); Larisa Muravska (Ukraine); Peda Zivotic (Yugoslavia).

• CONTENTS

Unit Four:

GETTING INVOLVED   189

Appendixes   239

INTRODUCTION

Environment and Our Global Community is based on a philosophy that can be easily communicated to young people and that will help them develop a value system consistent with the goals of creating and maintaining free and open societies. This curriculum emphasizes the themes of unity and community. Only when we truly understand that we are all united in one global community can we work together effectively to create a healthy environment for all life on the planet.

The philosophy of this curriculum is centered on spreading awareness and knowledge of the current environmental state of the Earth by unifying our families, our schools, our communities, our countries, our continents, and our planet, to work together. When we understand the vital role each of us has in making the world a better, healthier place, we can begin to understand the importance of environmental education. In accordance with that understanding, we must also recognize how our efforts affect what happens to others. By uniting and working together, we can create a healthy environment. As human beings, we are interconnected with other systems, beyond ourselves. We live in a world of nature, itself comprising many systems. What one of us does has an impact on other people and on the environment. We make decisions that affect all other living things, sometimes far beyond what we can see. If someone spills something harmful into a river, it is harmful to the creatures that live in the river and to all the people and creatures that depend on the river, even thousands of miles away. If we live in areas that are heavily polluted, that pollution affects the survival of all living things. If we cut down trees to make room for houses, factories, or roads, we change the environment for all the creatures that need those trees, and we change the environment overall. For these reasons, we must look at the effects of our actions on the environment through unity and community.

We are beginning the process of unity through the development of this internationally written curriculum. We have sought the unity of education coordinators from across diverse geographical boundaries and backgrounds. Together we've developed the philosophy that unifies our effort. Whether we see environmental education as a means to alleviate health problems, to remedy the scars of ecologically unsound political policies, to ensure the long-term economic viability of natural resources, or to preserve nature as a source of beauty, all the educational coordinators agree that the water we drink and the air we breathe are the earthly inheritance of our children—our future. And we've found unity in the means to create a better world community. In the teaching methods contained in this curriculum, we stress unity and community among students through excursions, contests, exhibitions, and—most importantly—dialogue. Through active participation and dialogue, students will discover cooperative learning, a life skill important not only in the classroom but also in the living room, the courtroom, and the community center, and across national borders. When students learn to prepare a presentation with fellow classmates, they will be taking the first step toward the exchange of information and ideas through a multitude of channels.

Combined with the themes of unity and community, we want to communicate positive thinking. Let's turn failure into success and inspire our students. Facing adversity without fear of failure, focusing on what we can do to overcome some of our environmental problems, let us together teach our children to believe in their own power and brighten their future through unity and community.

HOW TO USE THIS CURRICULUM

Environment and Our Global Community is a curriculum guide for classroom teachers who want to introduce environmental themes to middle school students. We have designed the curriculum to provide a flexible framework for the development of many environment-based concepts and activities. We want to empower students to use their own initiative to cope with environmental issues. Feel free to revise, adapt, and integrate the curriculum to meet their needs.

We encourage teacher-student and student-student interaction and interdependence. To be successful you should take students out of the classroom and involve them in the larger environment in which they live. Make connections with people in other schools, communities, and countries to share your knowledge, questions, and mutual interests.

Environment and Our Global Community is self-contained, providing a number of lessons and activities. We encourage you to add lesson plans and activities, add or update background information, and suggest additional ways to work with parents and the community. Because cultural differences exist, you should make changes to the curriculum to fit it into your community's cultural framework.

FORMAT

The curriculum is divided into four units: Community and Unity, Our Actions and Our Environment, Learning About Pollution, and Getting Involved. These hold the lesson plans and activities for teachers and students. Each lesson provides learning objectives, background information, materials, teacher tips, and activities with step-by-step directions for presentation. Some lessons include activity and resource pages that you can reproduce for classroom use. The curriculum is interdisciplinary. You can integrate the material into other subjects so that students learn that environmental issues are connected to all aspects of life.

UNIT ONE
Community and Unity:
Philosophy of Environmental Education

☙❧

UNDERSTANDING THE PHILOSOPHY OF ENVIRONMENTAL EDUCATION

OBJECTIVES

Upon completing this lesson, students will be able to

1. Identify the aspects of environmental education that will be important in their studies and

2. Understand the philosophy of this curriculum.

BACKGROUND

This curriculum is based on a holistic philosophy that emphasizes the themes of unity and community. Only when we work together as a global community can we create a healthy environment for all life on Earth. This activity provides an opportunity for students to work directly with the philosophy.

MATERIALS

The Flower resource sheet
Environmental Philosophy resource sheet (copies for each student)
Large sheet of paper (optional)
Tape

TEACHER TIPS

Prior to this lesson, review the information in the beginning of the curriculum on the philosophy of the program. This will help you understand the concept of the flower and the six dimensions of health.

PREPARATION

Write one of these words on each petal of The Flower resource sheet:

+ physical
+ mental
+ emotional
+ social
+ personal
+ spiritual

If you have a large class, you may want to redraw the flower on a larger sheet of paper so that all students can see the end product. Cut out each petal.

ACTIVITY

1. Explain to students that this curriculum is based on a holistic approach to environmental education. This means that environmental issues should be studied in the context of the complex relationships among human beings; among human beings and other living creatures of the planet; and among human beings, other living creatures, and the elements we all need to survive. We believe that all aspects of the planet are interrelated and interdependent. In the long run, anything that happens to one part of the planet affects all other parts, even if we do not see the direct correlation in our everyday lives.

2. Tell the students that in this activity they will begin to understand this philosophy and why it is important in this program and in their lives.

3. Ask the students to form six groups. Give each group a petal of the flower. Do not tell them what the paper represents. They will discover that at the end.

4. Ask each group to identify the important aspects of the environment that relate to the topic on their petal, and record their ideas. They may write words or draw pictures.

5. When the groups have completed their work, ask each group to share their ideas with the whole class. As they do, hang their petals in the form of a flower so they see the philosophy as a whole.

6. Summarize their ideas and the importance of understanding the interdependence of all six parts of the flower in all areas of education.

7. Distribute and discuss Environmental Philosophy resource sheet.

THE FLOWER

ENVIRONMENTAL PHILOSOPHY

When you read the philosophy of the flower, you can see how each petal is dependent on the others to make the flower whole. We must recognize the interdependence of each part on the others and the whole on each part. When you look at the need to study the environment, think of each aspect of the flower and how it relates to your life. But it doesn't only relate to you. Stretch your thinking. You need to think not only about how the flower relates to you but how you relate to the flower and to your world. We have a great deal of influence over what happens to all the communities and to the planet as a whole. Every action we take has consequences. Every river or stream we use affects life beyond ourselves. We are not isolated beings. We affect one another. Because of this, it is important to spread concern for and knowledge of the current environmental state of the Earth by unifying our families, our schools, our communities, our countries, our continents, and our PLANET.

DISCOVERING NATURE

OBJECTIVES

Upon completing this lesson, students will be able to

1. Discover surroundings through observation and

2. Become familiar with the nature of a small area of their neighborhood.

BACKGROUND

Direct contact is the best way of gaining knowledge. In this activity, students go outside to investigate a small area in order to observe its diversity. In this way they will better understand the natural world and their place in it.

MATERIALS

Discovering Nature activity sheet (copies for each student; see activity sheet for materials needed)
Discovering Nature data sheet (copies for each student)

TEACHER TIPS

Remind the students to wash their hands thoroughly after completing this activity.

PREPARATION

Choose an easily accessible area for the activity and make sure that it is free of poisonous plants and other potentially harmful materials.

ACTIVITY

1. Distribute Discovering Nature activity and data sheets and review. Divide the class into small groups and ask each group to choose a plot.

2. Tell groups the purpose of performing the activity is to become familiar with the nature that is around them.

3. Once the class is back in the classroom, ask each group to write a report on its plot and describe it to the class.

DISCOVERING NATURE

MATERIALS

meter stick

ball of string

large paper clips

thermometer

PROCEDURE

1. Enter the location of your plot on the Discovering Nature data sheet.

2. Mark off a 1-meter plot with the string using the paper clips to tack the string to the ground.

2. Use the thermometer to measure the temperature of the plot.

3. Observe the site and describe the condition of the light, ground, soil, and vegetation. Record them on the data sheet.

4. Record the animal and plant species found as well as any signs of human activity. Remember that anthills, wormholes, and chewed leaves are some of the signs that animals are or have been present.

DISCOVERING NATURE

PLOT LOCATION:

_____

PLOT CHARACTERISTICS:

Temperature: _____

Sunlight

_____in Sun   _____in light shade   _____in deep shade

Ground   **Soil**

____level   ____sloped   ____light brown   ____dark brown

____untrampled   ____trampled   ____light texture   ____heavy texture

Vegetation coverage

____light   ____heavy

Species found:

Plants:

_____   _____

_____   _____

_____   _____

_____   _____

_____   _____

_____   _____

_____   _____

Animals or signs of animals:

_____   _____

_____   _____

_____   _____

_____   _____

_____   _____

_____   _____

Signs of human activity:

_____   _____

_____   _____

_____   _____

_____   _____

_____   _____

_____   _____

A PLACE WHERE I FEEL HAPPY

OBJECTIVES

Upon completing this lesson, students will be able to

1. Identify aspects of different environments in which they feel comfortable,

2. Consider a variety of factors that could damage those places, and

3. Understand that the environment, no matter how large or small, can be changed in a variety of ways.

BACKGROUND

This activity allows students to begin to think about their own environment and what they want from their surroundings. There are important things to consider when studying the environment—things that relate to air and water pollution, habitats, the ozone layer, and climate. Students need to understand unity—that even places close to home are affected by what happens in other parts of the planet. They must also understand that what they do in one place has an effect on life in another place.

MATERIALS

Place Where I Feel Happy activity sheet (copies for each student)

TEACHER TIPS

After the students have completed this activity, suggest that they ask their parents what their favorite place is/was and if anything has happened to change it. This will allow parents to participate in this environment lesson and can help to make the point that one generation's behavior affects what future generations can experience.

ACTIVITY

1. Ask the students to remember a place that made them happy and list the characteristics of the place that made it wonderful.

2. Divide the class into pairs and ask students to share their list with their partners.

3. After a few minutes, ask the pairs to find another pair with which to exchange their lists.

4. Re-assemble the class and tell the students to think about what would make their place less pleasurable. Ask them to write about the changes they thought of and how those changes affected the place. Ask them to also write about their feelings now that the place has changed. Then have them find their original partner and discuss the place and their feelings about it now that it is different.

5. When the paired discussions are complete, lead a general discussion with the whole class. Ask several volunteers to describe their places and their feelings about their places before and after the changes.

6. Summarize the activity by noting that there are many favorite places that may be changed if we are not careful about how we affect the environment.

PLACE WHERE I FEEL HAPPY

PLACE THAT MADE ME HAPPY:

_____

Characteristics that made it wonderful:

1. _____

2. _____

3. _____

4. _____

5. _____

CHANGES THAT WOULD MAKE THE PLACE LESS PLEASURABLE	
Change	**How Change Affected My Place**
1.	
2.	
3.	
4.	
5.	

My feelings now that the place has changed:

_____

_____

MY DAY

OBJECTIVES

Upon completing this lesson, students will be able to recognize the impact of their actions on the environment.

BACKGROUND

This activity gives students a chance to be more conscious of the relationship between their actions and the environment in which they live. Please remember to be non-judgmental. Allowing the students to speak freely is the beginning of developing a trusting relationship. If we truly want to make changes in our environment, we must trust, and trust will affect the desire of the students to make change.

MATERIALS

What I Did Today activity sheet (copies for each student)

TEACHER TIPS

If students express powerlessness to change anything, reinforce the idea that we all affect the environment. Every drop of water that one young person conserves leaves water for the next person, for example. When students can understand their role in the environment, they can begin to understand that they too can make a positive difference.

ACTIVITY

DAY 1:

1. Suggest to the students that they may not be conscious of spending time in the environment. They may think of the environment as an abstract idea and not related to their daily activities. This activity is intended to bring the environment closer to home.

2. Distribute What I Did Today activity sheet. Ask the students to carry it with them during the following day to write down the things they do, from the time they wake up until they go to sleep, in the first column. Tell them to be very specific.

Day 2:

1. In class, ask the students to complete the second column, listing all the things they use doing the activities they noted in the first column. For example, if they mentioned taking the school bus, they should include "bus" and "fuel" in the second column. Ask them to think in specific detail.

2. Tell the students to think about how each of their activities may have affected the environment and note that in the third column. As they review each activity, ask them to think about the following questions:

   + Did your activities add to air or water pollution?

   + Did your activities involve the use of some form of energy?

   + Was the environment changed in some way by the activity?

3. Organize the class into groups of four or five. Tell them to discuss their lists and the potential consequences their actions may have on the environment. Then have each group brainstorm what they might do differently that would not affect the environment in a negative way or that might actually help the environment.

WHAT I DID TODAY

INSTRUCTIONS:

1. Write down the things you do, from the time you wake up until you go to sleep, in the first column. Be very specific.

2. In class, complete the second column, listing all the things you used doing the activities you noted in column one. Be very specific. For example, if you mentioned taking the school bus, include "bus" and "fuel" in the second column.

3. Review each activity and note in the last column how it affected the environment. Think about the following questions:

   • Did your activities add to air or water pollution?

   • Did your activities involve the use of some form of energy?

   • Was the environment changed in some way by the activity?

Time	Activity	Things used	How does this affect the environment?
6:00 AM			
7:00 AM			
8:00 AM			
9:00 AM			
10:00 AM			
11:00 AM			
NOON			
1:00 PM			
2:00 PM			
3:00 PM			
4:00 PM			
5:00 PM			
6:00 PM			
7:00 PM			
8:00 PM			
9:00 PM			
10:00 PM			
11:00 PM			
MIDNIGHT			

WHAT I COULD DO DIFFERENTLY
TO HELP THE ENVIRONMENT:

1. _____
_____
_____
_____

2. _____
_____
_____
_____

3. _____
_____
_____
_____

4. _____
_____
_____
_____

5. _____
_____
_____
_____

MY NEIGHBORHOOD

OBJECTIVES

Upon completing this lesson, students will be able to

1. Develop an environmentally detailed idea of their neighborhood and

2. Think about their neighborhood in different ways.

BACKGROUND

There are many things students may like about where they live—their community or neighborhood. There may also be things they would like to change. Encourage them to look closely at their local environment, as a way to become more aware of it and of what they can do to improve it. This will develop their sense of community.

MATERIALS

My Neighborhood activity sheet (copies for each student)
Crayons or drawing pencils
Large paper for the drawings
Tape

TEACHER TIPS

Ask students questions that encourage them to explore their thoughts and feelings—questions that begin with what, where, when, who, why, and how. Allow students to answer questions without placing judgment on them.

PREPARATION

Distribute My Neighborhood activity sheet. As a homework assignment, ask students to be very aware of everything about the environment in their neighborhood and community over the next three days. Ask them to complete the activity sheet, noting what they see, hear, smell, and touch.

ACTIVITY

1. Ask students to draw a map, diagram, or picture of their neighborhood based on the information they recorded on their activity sheets.

2. When the students have completed their work, ask them to hang the artwork around the room. Encourage them to walk around the room and look closely at the pictures so that they can ask questions about them and discuss what they see.

3. When all the students are seated, lead a general discussion about the artwork and the impressions the students created. Ask specific questions of the students to develop their own critical thinking and questioning skills. Encourage them to discuss how they feel about what they have seen. Suggestions for questions that allow students to explore their thoughts include:

   + Can you tell me more about your neighborhood?

   + How do you feel living there right now?

   + How would your neighborhood look if it were exactly as you would like it to be?

   + What's most important for you in your neighborhood?

   + How do you see things changing?

4. As you bring the activity to an end, ask students to begin to imagine what they might want to change and what they could do, individually, in groups, or as a whole class, to make a positive difference in their local environment.

5. Save the activity sheets and artwork for use in Building a Sense of Community (Part 2).

MY NEIGHBORHOOD

What I Saw	Where
1.	
2.	
3.	
4.	
5.	

What I Heard	Where
1.	
2.	
3.	
4.	
5.	

What I Smelled	Where
1.	
2.	
3.	
4.	
5.	

What I Touched	Where
1.	
2.	
3.	
4.	
5.	

BUILDING A SENSE OF COMMUNITY
(PART 1)

OBJECTIVES

Upon completing this lesson, students will be able to

1. Examine the idea of community as it relates to environment concepts and

2. Understand the connections among many parts of the environment, not just human beings.

BACKGROUND

Most humans live in communities in which they interact with each other to meet their needs. When we think of communities, we usually think of people, but non-living elements are important parts of communities as well. Without minerals, air, water, and Sun, there would be no human community. Yet we often take these things for granted. Part of the purpose of this curriculum is to help students be more conscious of the elements on which humans and other living creatures depend. With that awareness will come the realization that we must care for and conserve the elements essential to our existence.

MATERIALS

Large sheets of paper
Markers

TEACHER TIPS

This activity may take two or three class periods. The more the students discuss and sort their own definitions, the more clearly they will understand the needs within their own communities. It then becomes possible to reach out into the environment.

ACTIVITY

1. Divide the class into small groups and ask the groups to define community. They may be unsure about what you mean and what you want. That's okay. Let them struggle with the concept in their groups.

2. After 10 minutes, ask the groups to share their definitions. Ask them to identify the points they think are most important. When all have reported, see if there is one definition on

which the class can agree—one that has the important elements of community. Most likely students will not mention the essential non-living elements:

+ minerals
+ air
+ water
+ Sun

Praise the students for their thinking, then suggest that there are things that humans need that are not human or created by humans. Ask if they know what these things are. If they do not name the four elements after a few minutes, ask questions that will lead them to these elements.

3. Ask the students to form four groups. Each group represents one of the non-living essentials for life. Ask the students in each group to identify the ways in which that element is essential to living creatures, and write their responses on large sheets of paper. When the groups have completed their work, ask each to share what they have discovered.

4. Tell the class that animals also need these elements. As we, humans, use animals or affect them, we affect the lives of other living creatures, not just ourselves. Remind the students that humans have the ability to affect all other living things and so we have a large responsibility to take care of them. You may want to end the activity by emphasizing the interconnectedness of all creatures.

BUILDING A SENSE OF COMMUNITY (PART 2)

OBJECTIVES

Upon completing this lesson, students will be able to expand their ideas of what exists in their neighborhood and in the environment in general.

BACKGROUND

This activity expands the concept of community. Students may have identified the obvious things in their neighborhood—those things that humans created. There is value in asking them to consider those things that humans did not create but that affect humans and other living creatures nevertheless.

MATERIALS

Completed My Neighborhood activity sheets and artwork (from My Neighborhood, page 24)
Environmental Terms resource sheet (copies for each student)

TEACHER TIPS

If you have the time and resources, take your students to a natural community (ecosystem) and have them observe the interactions among the parts. Getting students out into the environment, as a group, can be a wonderful way to reinforce the concepts important to this curriculum.

ACTIVITY

1. Ask students to review their completed My Neighborhood activity sheets from My Neighborhood.

2. When they are finished, ask if there are specific things that they think they need to add, based on the previous lesson.

3. Define and discuss ecosystem (an integrated unit consisting of the living organisms and the physical environment in a particular area). Ask the students to identify the ecosystems in their neighborhood. They may say forests, ponds, lakes, dead trees, and other examples.

4. Form the students into small groups, each one representing a natural community the class has identified. Ask each group to identify the living things that inhabit that ecosystem and how they interact with each other to form communities and sustain life. Suggest that they think about how the living things get food, water, shelter, and air in that community. Once the groups have finished, re-assemble the class and have each group present its work.

5. Distribute Environmental Terms resource sheet and discuss the terms. Remember to emphasize the concepts of interdependence and interconnectedness.

6. Ask the students to look at their artwork from My Neighborhood and label each part according to the definitions.

ENVIRONMENTAL TERMS

community: an interacting population of various kinds of individuals in a common location.

ecology: the study of the relationship between living things and their physical environment.

ecosystem: an integrated unit consisting of the living organisms and the physical environment in a particular area. For example, an oak tree, with all the creatures that live within it, is an ecosystem.

habitat: the place or type of site where a plant or animal naturally or normally lives and grows.

population: a group of creatures of the same species that are in sufficiently close contact to enable the different individuals to interbreed.

species: a class of organisms having common attributes and designated by a common name; members of a species can mate and produce offspring.

MY COMMUNITY: PAST–PRESENT–FUTURE

OBJECTIVES

Upon completing this lesson, students will be able to

1. Make connections between the past, present, and future status of their local environment;

2. Understand that a study of the environment can be made over time; and

3. Explore issues of the environment with their families.

BACKGROUND

Communities change. Some people move out and others move in. Some species move or die out and others move in. To have a sense of what a community—natural and human—used to be can provide an interesting perspective on the current environment. Change from the past may provide a valuable perspective about the potential for change in the future.

MATERIALS

My Community activity sheet (copies for each student)

TEACHER TIPS

You may want to ask the students to collect old photographs or other information illustrating what their interviews described.

ACTIVITY

1. Explain to the students that they will be exploring how their communities may have changed.

2. Distribute My Community activity sheet. Ask the students to use the boxes marked "Past," "Present," and "Future" to illustrate, either in words or in drawings, their views of their community as it has changed over time.

3. Tell the students to develop questions they might ask people in their families and in the larger community about what the community used to be like and write their questions on the activity sheet. Then ask them to list with whom in their family or neighborhood

they might discuss these questions. As a homework assignment, give them a few days to interview the people they have chosen.

4. At the end of that time, ask them to share their findings with the class.

MY COMMUNITY

Past	Present	Future (10 years from now)

Questions to ask my family or neighbors about how my community has changed:

1. _____
2. _____
3. _____
4. _____
5. _____

Who I will ask:

1. _____
2. _____
3. _____

INTERVIEWS

Interview 1 (name): _____

Answer to question:

1. _____
   _____

2. _____
   _____

3. _____
   _____

4. _____
   _____

5. _____
   _____

Interview 2 (name): _____

Answer to question:

1. _____
   _____

2. _____
   _____

3. _____
   _____

4. _____
   _____

5. _____
   _____

Interview 3 (name): _____

Answer to question:

1. _____
   _____

2. _____
   _____

3. _____
   _____

4. _____
   _____

5. _____
   _____

DECLARATION OF RESPONSIBILITY TO NATURE

OBJECTIVES

Upon completing this lesson, students will be able to

1. Look at nature from a different perspective and

2. Write a Declaration of Responsibility to Nature.

BACKGROUND

Many questions related to the environment involve ethical, moral, and values issues. They entail making decisions and choices and solving problems that affect us and other people—people we may not know, people in generations to come. People may find it difficult to see beyond today, especially when they are facing the challenges of economic, social, and political change. But when it comes to matters that affect the environment, we must think beyond today and see the global interconnectedness of our world. Identifying with nature is of great importance because it helps students look at nature from a different perspective based on understanding, identification, and responsibility to the environment. It makes students think consciously about moral problems such as: What real needs do I have? Do I have the right to rule over nature? Is my behavior toward nature responsible?

MATERIALS

If I Were activity sheet (copies for each student)
Declaration of Responsibility to Nature activity sheet (copies for each student)

TEACHER TIPS

This activity is appropriate for younger students. Provoke the students to discussions after each activity. This will help them think the subject over and discover new values.

ACTIVITY

1. Distribute and ask the students to complete If I Were activity sheet.

2. Divide the students into groups of four and tell the students to share their answers with the other members of the group. Distribute Declaration of Responsibility to Nature activity sheet and ask each group to brainstorm a declaration based on their discussion.

3. Have each group write a declaration of responsibility and ask each student to think of one person he or she would like to send it to and why.

IF I WERE

Instructions:
Complete the following statements and then determine what environmental problems you might face as that object:

If I were a stone, I would like to be a_____because _____
_____

The problems I might face include:
_____
_____

If I were water, I would like to be_____because _____
_____

The problems I might face include:
_____
_____

If I were a tree, I would like to be a_____because _____
_____

The problems I might face include:
_____
_____

If I were an animal, I would like to be a_____because _____
_____

The problems I might face include:
_____
_____

Activity sheets may be downloaded from www.idebate.org/environment.htm.

DECLARATION OF RESPONSIBILITY TO NATURE

We declare that we are responsible to nature in the following ways:

_____
_____
_____
_____
_____
_____
_____
_____
_____
_____

I want to send my declaration to:

Name: _____

Address: _____
_____

I think it will affect him or her in the following ways:

_____
_____
_____
_____
_____
_____
_____

Activity sheets may be downloaded from www.idebate.org/environment.htm.

UNIT TWO
Our Actions and Our Environment:
How We Make a Difference

CRSO

ENVIRONMENTAL SURVEY

OBJECTIVES

Upon completing this lesson, students will be able to

1. Explore the reasons for learning about the environment and

2. Discuss their role in preserving the environment.

BACKGROUND

Students are most involved in the learning process when they understand the relevance of the subject to themselves. Children often think of environmental issues as belonging to other people, especially adults they do not know. This activity will help students explore the importance of environmental education in their own world as well as in the larger world around them.

MATERIALS

Activity 1: None
Activity 2: Environmental Survey activity sheet (copies for each student)

TEACHER TIPS

Adapt the survey to the environmental conditions in your community.

ACTIVITY

ACTIVITY 1: WHY ENVIRONMENTAL EDUCATION IS IMPORTANT

Form the class into small groups of five to seven and ask each group to consider the following questions:

+ Why should I study about the environment?

+ What does environmental education mean to me?

Ask them to write their ideas on large sheets of paper. Give them 15 minutes and then ask each group to share its ideas with the whole class. You may summarize the discussion, emphasizing the subjects you and the students will be studying and the concepts that are most important.

ACTIVITY 2: ENVIRONMENTAL SURVEY

Distribute Environmental Survey activity sheet and ask each student to complete it. When the survey is completed, ask the students to form small groups and discuss their responses. Ask them to identify any questions they think are important for the whole class to discuss.

ENVIRONMENTAL SURVEY

When I am the last person to leave a room in my house, I turn the lights off.	YES	NO
When I brush my teeth, I turn the water off until I finish.	YES	NO
My family always makes sure the dishwasher is full before we use it.	YES	NO
My family and I reuse or recycle glass bottles.	YES	NO
I have helped to plant a tree.	YES	NO
My family donates used clothes and toys.	YES	NO
When I'm cold at home, I ____put on a sweater OR ____turn up the heat. (check one answer)		
I volunteer to help neighborhood cleanup drives.	YES	NO
I like to read books or magazine articles about the Earth.	YES	NO
During the day I ____sit next to a window to read OR ____turn on a light if it is too dark to read. (check one answer)		
My family composts food waste.	YES	NO
In the winter my family closes the curtains to keep the cold out and the heat in.	YES	NO
Whenever possible, I use recycled paper.	YES	NO
When I'm hungry, I____ open the refrigerator door to see what there is to eat, OR ____I think about what I want to eat before I open the refrigerator. (check one answer)		
The napkins we use at home are made of ____cloth OR ____paper. (check one answer)		
When traveling to school, I usually ____take the school bus or public transportation, ____walk, OR ____get a ride from my friends or folks. (check one answer)		
When I see paper or other trash on the sidewalk, I ____stop to pick it up OR ____ ignore it and continue walking. (check one answer)		
My family recycles paper.	YES	NO
My family pours household cleaners or paint down the drain.	YES	NO
If I bring my lunch to school, I carry it in a ____cloth bag, ____paper bag, OR ____ metal lunch box. (check one answer)		
I have talked to my parents about the environment.	YES	NO
I usually take a ____shower OR a ____bath. (check one answer)		
When I want a drink of cold water, I ____let the water run until it's really cold, OR I ____keep a container of water in the refrigerator. (check one answer)		

I ____ let water run in the sink while I wash and rinse the dishes, OR ____ I put soapy water in one side of the sink or in one container and water for rinsing the dishes in another. (check one answer)		
I am careful to pick only those wildflowers that are plentiful and that are not protected by law.	YES	NO
I have written a letter to a local newspaper about an environmental topic.	YES	NO
I try to set a good environmental example for others.	YES	NO

Activity sheets may be downloaded from www.idebate.org/environment.htm.

WASTE AT HOME

OBJECTIVES

Upon completing this lesson, students will be able to

1. Identify the many different types of household waste and

2. Identify the appropriate methods of waste management.

BACKGROUND

Our handling of waste affects our community in many ways. Many of the products we throw in the garbage do not decay properly and can spread diseases. Chemical substances, medicines, and coloring agents that people place in the trash or flush down the toilet pollute the environment. Plastic bags and other materials can threaten animal life, if not discarded properly. This activity teaches students that they can do something to prevent unnecessary pollution in their daily lives and shows them how solid wastes can be handled in environmentally acceptable ways.

MATERIALS

Activity 1: Waste Checklist activity sheet (copies for each student)
Activity 2: Trash List
Managing Solid Waste resource sheet (copies for each student)

TEACHER TIPS

Modify the Trash List in Activity 2 to reflect your students' lifestyle.

ACTIVITY

ACTIVITY 1: HOME WASTE

1. Lead a discussion about reusable and recyclable waste in your students' daily lives. You may suggest some examples such as plastic, paper, glass, aluminum, etc.

2. As a homework assignment, have the students complete Waste Checklist activity sheet, weighing their trash and dividing the waste they find in their home into reuse, recycle, and toss.

3. After the class has completed the assignment, ask the students to calculate how much trash the their families would generate in a month, in a year. Assuming that the families of each student in the school averaged the same amount of trash, how much trash would all families generate in a year?

4. Compile a master list from the Reuse, Recycle, Toss tables in Part II of the activity sheet and ask the students to develop ways of limiting the waste they cannot reuse or recycle.

ACTIVITY 2: MANAGING SOLID WASTE

Preparation

Print one term from the Trash List in Activity 2 on an index card and tack each card to the chalkboard in random order.

1. Distribute Managing Solid Waste resource sheet and discuss the five ways of managing solid waste:

2. Form the class into five teams, each representing one way to manage solid waste. Have one member from each team approach the board and select a card with a "piece of trash" appropriate for the member's team. After the first team member chooses an item, the remaining members of the team take turns choosing. Students may consult with their team members to make the choice.

3. Once the students have chosen all the items, ask each team to name the item it has chosen and explain why.

WASTE CHECKLIST

PART I: FAMILY TRASH

Over the next week weigh your family's trash. (Weigh yourself and then weigh yourself holding a trash bag. Be sure to include all the trash, including newspapers, magazines, bottles, cartons, etc.) Record the weight in the table below.

Day	Trash Weight
1.	
2.	
3.	
4.	
5.	
6.	
7.	
Week Total	

PART II: REUSE, RECYCLE, TOSS

Over the next week, inspect your family's trash and put each item in the appropriate category below.

Reuse	Recycle	Toss
1.	1.	1.
2.	2.	2.
3.	3.	3.
4.	4.	4.
5.	5.	5.
6.	6.	6.
7.	7.	7.
8.	8.	8.
9.	9.	9.
10.	10.	10.

Activity sheets may be downloaded from www.idebate.org/environment.htm.

Trash List

Aluminum foil
Apple or orange peel
Automobile tire
Automotive antifreeze
Battery
Book
Brown paper bag
Cell phone
CD
Chair
Coffee grounds
Corrugated cardboard box
Dental floss
Dried leaves
Egg shell
Food scraps
Glass or glass jar
Light bulb
Milk carton
Newspaper
Paint
Paper clip
Peach pit
Pencil
Plastic soda bottle
Rubber band
Scrap iron
Sweater
Used facial tissue

Activity sheets may be downloaded from www.idebate.org/environment.htm.

MANAGING SOLID WASTE

THE FIVE WAYS TO MANAGE SOLID WASTE

1. **Source reduction and reuse**—reusing or extending the life of products and shrinking the amount we throw out by using fewer toxic materials and changing the design, manufacture, or use of products.

2. **Recycling**—mining valuable materials out of garbage to make new products.

3. **Composting**—recycling organics like yard trimmings and food scraps through decomposition.

4. **Waste-to-energy**—burning municipal solid waste in a controlled environment to create steam or electricity.

5. **Sanitary landfills**—used when the other four methods are not appropriate.

Activity sheets may be downloaded from www.idebate.org/environment.htm.

HOME ENERGY AUDIT

OBJECTIVES

Upon completing this lesson, students will be able to extend their new awareness of energy consumption and explore options for reducing consumption.

BACKGROUND

The typical U.S. family spends almost $1,300 a year on their home's utility bills. Unfortunately, a large portion of that energy is wasted through poor insulation, use of energy inefficient appliances, etc. Because we usually generate energy through the burning of fossil fuels that put toxic gases and particles into the air, we can help the environment and save money by making our homes more energy efficient. This lesson helps students understand this concept by viewing their homes as an energy system with interdependent parts.

MATERIALS

Home Energy Audit activity sheet (copies for each student)

TEACHER TIPS

The audit mentions the ENERGY STAR® label, given to appliances that the U.S. Environmental Protection Agency and Department of Energy have identified as being the most energy efficient products in their classes. For more information on the program go to http://www.energystar.gov.

ACTIVITY

1. Distribute Home Energy Audit activity sheet and ask the students to work with their parents to complete the audit.

2. Ask students to form groups to discuss how to make their homes more energy efficient.

HOME ENERGY AUDIT

INSTRUCTIONS:

Complete the following audit to determine how energy efficient your home is. You may need your parents' help in answering some of the questions.

INSULATION AND WEATHERIZATION

1. Are the following insulated?

   • Exterior walls_____

   • Attic_____

   • Basement walls_____

   • Crawl spaces_____

2. Are the following weatherized to prevent warm air from leaking into your home during the summer and out of your home during the winter?

   • Attic hatches_____

   • Ceiling fixtures_____

   • Doors_____

   • Electrical boxes and outlets_____

   • Plumbing fixtures_____

   • Windows_____

LIGHTING

1. Does my home use energy efficient fluorescent bulbs wherever possible? _____Yes _____No

2. Does my home use ENERGY STAR® qualified lighting (lighting that meets the highest government standards for energy efficiency)? _____Yes _____No

MAJOR ELECTRICAL APPLIANCES						
Appliance	**Very Light Use**				**Very Heavy Use**	**Has the appliance earned the ENERGY STAR® or is it energy efficient?**
	1	2	3	4	5	
						____Yes ____No ____Don't know
						____Yes ____No ____Don't know
						____Yes ____No ____Don't know
						____Yes ____No ____Don't know
						____Yes ____No ____Don't know
						____Yes ____No ____Don't know
						____Yes ____No ____Don't know
						____Yes ____No ____Don't know
						____Yes ____No ____Don't know
						____Yes ____No ____Don't know
						____Yes ____No ____Don't know

APPLIANCE AUDIT

OBJECTIVES

Upon completing this lesson, students will be able to understand how the increase in household appliances has contributed to the greater demand for energy.

BACKGROUND

The number of appliances in our homes has increased dramatically over the past decades. Electric pizza warmers, bread makers, battery chargers, and eyeglass cleaners were unknown years ago; yet they are now common in many households. These appliances all use energy, which is in short supply and increasingly costly. Decreasing the number of appliances can help us save energy. It will also help the environment by limiting pollution (a result of energy generation) and waste (a result of our "throwaway society").

MATERIALS

Appliance Checklist (copies for each student)

TEACHER TIPS

Students may think that *appliance* means only stoves, ovens, etc. Point out that we now have many specialized appliances and give some examples. Also remind them to check in closets, drawers, and cupboards for appliances during their audit.

ACTIVITY

1. Distribute Appliance Checklist and ask the students to complete it in class.

2. As a homework assignment ask the students to go through each room of their house and add other appliances they find. When they complete the assignment, ask them were they surprised at the number of appliances they didn't know they had.

3. Tell them to ask their parents to indicate what appliances they had when they were the students' age. If possible have the students ask their grandparents or older adults to indicate what appliances they had.

4. When the audits are completed, tell the students to graph appliance use over the three generations.

5. Ask the students to review their audits and indicate which appliances they must have and which they could eliminate.

APPLIANCE CHECKLIST

INSTRUCTIONS:

1. Conduct an appliance audit of your home, recording the number of each appliance you have in column 1.

2. Ask your parents to fill in column 2.

3. Ask your grandparents or other older adult to fill in column 3.

4. Review your list and indicate which appliance you must have and which you can eliminate.

	Appliances my family has	Appliances my parents had at my age	Appliances my grandparents had at my age	Must have	Don't need
air conditioner					
air purifier					
appliance timer					
bag sealer					
bagel slicer					
battery charger					
blanket					
blender					
boom box					
bottle warmer					
bread maker					
bun warmer					
can opener					
CD player					
cell phone charger					
coffeemaker					

	Appliances my family has	Appliances my parents had at my age	Appliances my grandparents had at my age	Must have	Don't need
computer					
computer monitor					
computer printer					
convection oven					
cookie baker					
crockpot					
curling iron					
deep fryer					
dehumidifier					
dehydrator					
dishwasher					
drill					
dryer					
egg cooker					
espresso machine					
eyeglass cleaner					
fan					
floor polisher					
fondue maker					
food mill					
food processor					
foot massager					
freezer					
furnace					
garbage disposal					
griddle					
grill					
guitar					
hair dryer					
heating pad					

	Appliances my family has	Appliances my parents had at my age	Appliances my grandparents had at my age	Must have	Don't need
hedge trimmer					
hot chocolate maker					
hot dog cooker					
humidifier					
ice cream maker					
ice shaver					
iron					
juicer					
karaoke equipment					
keyboard					
knife					
lamp					
massager					
microwave					
mixer					
nailer					
panini maker					
paper shredder					
pasta maker					
pencil sharpener					
pizza maker					
popcorn popper					
potato peeler					
pressure cooker					
quesadilla & tortilla maker					
radiator					
radio					
refrigerator					
rice cooker					

	Appliances my family has	Appliances my parents had at my age	Appliances my grandparents had at my age	Must have	Don't need
rug shampooer					
salad maker					
sewing machine					
skillet					
smoothie maker					
stereo					
stove					
tape deck					
television					
toaster oven					
toothbrush					
vacuum cleaner					
warmer tray					
water cooler					
water filter					
whirlpool tub					
wok					
yogurt maker					
OTHER					

WATER CONSUMPTION AT HOME

OBJECTIVES

Upon completing this lesson, students will be able to

1. Identify the leading sources of water use in American homes,

2. Name the purposes for which they use water, and

3. Develop a plan for reduction of water consumption.

BACKGROUND

Water is the most common substance found on Earth. Approximately 75% of the Earth's surface is water; yet less than 1% of that water is available for human use. We cannot afford to waste water, but we do so all the time. A lot of water waste occurs in the home. For example, a single dripping faucet can waste 283 to 378 liters of water per week. This activity will acquaint students with the need to reduce water consumption at home.

MATERIALS

Activity 1: Water Use Facts activity sheet (copies for each student)
Activity 2: Home Water Saver Audit activity sheet (copies for each student)
Water Usage Chart data sheet (copies for each student)
Activity 3: Liter containers to demonstrate 30 liters
Future Water activity sheets (copies for each student)

TEACHER TIPS

Activity 1 is appropriate for younger students.

In discussing the students' plans for conserving water, emphasize these five key tips:

    1. Check your water-using appliances and devices for leaks.

    2. Replace your old toilet, the largest water user in your house.

    3. Replace your clothes washer with an energy efficient model.

    4. Plant the right garden plants for your area.

    5. Water your plants only when necessary.

ACTIVITY

ACTIVITY 1: WATER USE

1. Distribute and ask the students to complete Water Use Facts.

2. Use the activity sheet to generate a discussion about how our society uses water in our daily lives.

ACTIVITY 2: HOME WATER SAVER AUDIT

1. As a homework assignment, ask the students to complete the Home Water Saver Audit activity sheet.

2. In class create a master list by room. Divide the students into groups, one group for each room. Ask each group to use their audits and Water Usage Chart to brainstorm ways to reduce water consumption in their room. Have each group share their ideas with the class.

3. Encourage students to share their plans with their family members and report to the class in your next session about the families' reactions.

ACTIVITY 3: FUTURE WATER

1. Propose the following problem for discussion: *Imagine that in 2025 there will be only 30 liters of water per person daily. How should it be used?*

You may need to present 30 liters visually to students. You can do this by having containers, either empty or full, representing 30 liters.

2. Develop this activity by asking students:

   + Do you think this question is realistic?

   + How would you feel if you didn't have the water you need for drinking? Washing?

   + What have you learned about wasting water?

   + Do you think you, as an individual, have an effect on the future of our water availability?

   + What role do you think each of us should take to prevent a water shortage in the year 2025?

WATER USE FACTS

Draw a line matching the items on the left to the amount of water on the right.

1. Taking a shower	A. 30 gallons
2. Watering the lawn	B. 180 gallons
3. Washing the dishes	C. 4–7 gallons
4. Washing clothes	D. 1/2 gallon
5. Flushing the toilet	E. 39,090 gallons
6. Brushing teeth	F. 62,600 gallons
7. Drinking	G. 15–30 gallons
8. Needed to produce one ton of steel	H. 9.3 gallons
9. Needed to process one can of fruit or vegetables	I. 1 gallon
10. Needed to manufacture a new car and its four tires	J. 9–20 gallons

Activity sheets may be downloaded from www.idebate.org/environment.htm.

WATER USE FACTS

1. Taking a shower — G. 15–30 gallons

2. Watering the lawn — B. 180 gallons

3. Washing the dishes — J. 9–20 gallons

4. Washing clothes — A. 30 gallons

5. Flushing the toilet — C. 4–7 gallons

6. Brushing teeth — I. 1 gallon

7. Drinking — D. 1/2 gallon

8. Needed to produce one ton of steel — F. 62,600 gallons

9. Needed to process one can of fruit or vegetables — H. 9.3 gallons

10. Needed to manufacture a new car and its four tires — E. 39,090 gallons

Source: U.S. Environmental Protection Agency, *Drinking Water and Ground Water Kid's Stuff*, http://www.epa.gov/safewater/kids/grades_4-8_matching_game_answers.html.

HOME WATER SAVER AUDIT

Room	What Uses Water?
Bath	
Garden	
Kitchen	
Laundry	

Room	What Uses Water?
Garage & Basement	
Garden	

WATER USAGE CHART

NATIONAL INDOOR PER CAPITA USE (PERCENT BY FIXTURE)	
Toilet	26.7
Washing machine	21.7
Shower	16.8
Faucet	15.7
Leaks	13.7
Bath	1.7
Dishwasher	1.4
Other domestic use	2.2

Source: California Urban Water Conservation Council, *H20 Water Saver Home*, http://www.h2ouse.org/tour/index.cfm; adapted from Mayer, P. W., W. B. DeOreo, E. Opitz, J. Kiefer, B. Dziegielewski, W. Davis, and J. O. Nelson, *Residential End Uses of Water* (Denver: American Water Works Association Research Foundation, 1999).

Activity sheets may be downloaded from www.idebate.org/environment.htm.

FUTURE WATER

Imagine that in 2025 there will be only 30 liters of water per person daily.

PART I:

Write a paragraph describing how it should be used.

PART II:

Answer the following questions:

1. Do you think this question is realistic?

2. How would you feel if you didn't have the water you need for drinking? Washing?

3. What have you learned about wasting water?

4. Do you think you, as an individual, have an effect on the future of our water availability?

5. What role do you think each of us should take to prevent a water shortage in the year 2025?

School Waste

OBJECTIVES

Upon completing this lesson the students will be able to

1. Identify key factors that lead to waste in school,

2. Identify the components of their school garbage, and

3. Apply waste reduction techniques to school garbage.

BACKGROUND

Schools are often a major source of waste. Students use—and throw away—enormous amounts of paper, and the disposable lunches they carry create a significant amount of garbage. It is estimated that the average person in the United States uses about 580 pounds of paper and that the average school-age child bringing a disposable lunch generates 67 pounds of waste per school year. Much of this is a result of using overpackaged foods, plastic bags, juice boxes and pouches, paper napkins, and disposable utensils. In this activity, the students will see how their lifestyle contributes to school waste, and they will develop ideas to help their school solve its waste problem.

MATERIALS

Activity 1: Paper Usage activity sheet (copies for each student)
Paper Process activity sheet (copies for each student)
Scale
Two paper-recycling bins
Yard stick
Activity 2: Lunch Waste activity sheet (copies for each student)

TEACHER TIPS

Activity 1: You may want to ask the student to graph the results of the week's paper use.

ACTIVITY

ACTIVITY 1: WASTE PAPER

Preparation
Label one of the paper-recycling bins "Completely Used" and the other "One Side."

1. Tell the students that for the next week they are to save all the paper they generate during the day and place it in one of the two bins. The bin marked "Completely Used" is for paper that they have used on both sides. The bin marked "One Side" is for paper that is blank on the second side.

2. At the end of each day have the class weigh and measure each stack and record the figures on Paper Usage activity sheet. (Remember to remind the class to subtract the weight of the bin from the total weight.)

3. At the end of the week, ask the students to calculate the total weight and height of each stack.

4. Distribute Paper Process activity sheet and ask students to note the effects each step in the process might have on the environment. Discuss the suggested effects with the entire class.

5. Lead a discussion on "Are we wasting paper?" and ask the class to brainstorm ways in which they might use paper more wisely.

Activity 2: Lunchroom Waste

1. Tell the students that for the next week they are to note everything left over from their lunch on Lunch Waste activity sheet. This includes cans and bottles, all packaging, food wrappers, paper napkins, leftover food, etc. They are then to indicate whether the item can be reused, recycled, or composted, or must be sent to a landfill. If the student brings the same item for several days, he is to note the number of times he brings it in the appropriate column. For example, if he brings a soda can each day, he will note 5 in the recycle column.

2. At the end of the week, ask the students to add up the total number of items in each column.

3. Have the students find the class total for each column.

4. Ask the class to brainstorm ways of reducing waste and tell the students to think of alternatives to current items and note them on the activity sheet.

PAPER USAGE

AMOUNT OF PAPER DISCARDED						
	Monday	Tuesday	Wednesday	Thursday	Friday	TOTAL
One side						
Height						
Weight						
Completely used						
Height						
Weight						

PAPER PROCESS

TREES

LOGGING

TRUCK TRANSPORTATION

PROCESSING AND PRODUCTION

WAREHOUSING

STORE

Activity sheets may be downloaded from www.idebate.org/environment.htm.

LUNCH WASTE

INSTRUCTIONS:

1. For the next week note everything left over from your lunch each day. This includes cans and bottles, all packaging, food wrappers, paper napkins, leftover food, etc.

2. Indicate whether the item can be reused, recycled, or composted, or must be sent to a landfill. If you bring the same item for several days, note the number of times in the appropriate column. For example, if you bring a soda can each day, note 5 in the recycle column.

3. At the end of the week, add up the total number in each column.

4. Think of an alternative for all items that cannot be reused.

Lunch Item	Reuse	Recycle	Compost	Landfill	Alternative
TOTAL					

Activity sheets may be downloaded from www.idebate.org/environment.htm.

ENVIRONMENTAL DEBATE

OBJECTIVES

Upon completing this lesson, students will be able to

1. Organize important information on an environmental issue,

2. Present their ideas in a clear and concise manner, and

3. Argue their case to try to convince others of their point of view.

BACKGROUND

Many environmental issues may seem far away to students; that is, they may seem to concern other people in other places. Participating in a debate can bring some of those issues closer to home and can generate enthusiasm for addressing matters that may then appear more relevant to the students. Knowing how to organize information, select information that is most important and convincing, and present ideas clearly and thoughtfully are all important skills students need to develop. This activity is intended to help develop those skills.

MATERIALS

Twenty Environmental Topics for Debate resource sheet
Karl Popper Debate Format resource sheet
Resource and reference materials needed for research

TEACHER TIPS

You may want to have all students participate as debaters or you may decide to have each group select a few people who will debate. Either way, all students should be involved in the research and the development of arguments and be ready to step into a debate situation.

ACTIVITY

1. Explain that you want your students to become critical thinkers—you want them to make decisions that are supported by accurate information, and to develop the skills needed to use the information wisely. Participating in a debate is one way to develop those skills.

2. Ask the students to think of the important environmental issues that affect their community and write these on the chalkboard. If necessary, refer to Twenty Environmental Debate Topics for more issues.

3. Ask the students to vote on the topics they would be interested in debating. (The number of topics you choose will depend on how much time you want to spend on this activity. Research involves significant time, and each debate will take a class period.) Once the students have chosen the topics, ask them to work in small groups to develop a debate statement. It must be clear and to the point. Some examples include the following:

    +   Although it is important to protect rain forests, the resources that come from them are too valuable for us to stop using.

    +   Even though protecting endangered species may affect the economy of countries in which some people depend on those animals to make money, protecting endangered species must take priority.

    +   The pollution caused by burning some fuels is less important than the money saved by using those fuels instead of others.

4. If you will be staging several debates, ask the students to select the issue and the side on which they want to work, or you could assign sides randomly. (In the format we are suggesting, you will need six students per topic—three for the affirmative; three for the negative.)

5. Determine the amount of research time you want the class to devote to the activity and discuss research procedures with the students.

6. You may use any debate format that is appropriate for your class, or you may conduct an informal debate. We have included the format and speaker responsibilities for the Karl Popper format used by the International Debate Education Association.

7. On the day of the debate, arrange the seats so that the debaters face the rest of the class.

8. Review the rules of the debate format with the students. You may decide to allow questions from the audience, directed to one or both sides. You may want to judge the debate or have the students not participating in the debate do so. Remember that if there is judging, it must be fair and unbiased, with the judge or judges focused on the arguments presented in the debate and not on which students they like most or with which side of the argument they agree. Judges must be able to explain their decision. This will help them and the other students understand what made one team's arguments more convincing than the other's.

TWENTY ENVIRONMENTAL TOPICS FOR DEBATE

1. Economic development is more important than environmental protection.

2. It is environmentally irresponsible to continue a lifestyle that depends on cars.

3. Environmental groups care more about the environment than people.

4. Environmental education should be mandatory for all students.

5. What is good for nature and the Earth is good for people.

6. Agriculture plays no part in environmental pollution.

7. We must move from fossil fuels to alternative sources of energy.

8. Industry can be both environmentally responsible and profitable.

9. We can solve most environmental problems through legislation.

10. It is government's responsibility to protect the environment.

11. We can solve environmental problems only by thinking globally.

12. Suburbs and rural areas are environmentally friendly; only cities pollute.

13. Environmental protection should be left to professionals.

14. Our consumer society is dangerous for the environment.

15. The international community should impose severe penalties on developing countries that pollute the atmosphere and destroy their forests.

16. Parents must take responsibility for their children's actions toward the environment.

17. Since species have become extinct throughout Earth's history, we do not need endangered species laws.

18. Students cannot effect environmental change.

19. Global warming is an illusion.

20. Environmental problems are exaggerated.

KARL POPPER DEBATE FORMAT

Karl Popper Debate Format		
Section	**Time**	**Speaker**
1. Affirmative Constructive	6 minutes	First Affirmative Speaker
2. Cross-Examination	3 minutes	Third Negative Speaker questions First Affirmative Speaker answers
3. Negative Constructive	6 minutes	First Negative Speaker
4. Cross-Examination	3 minutes	Third Affirmative Speaker questions First Negative Speaker answers
5. First Affirmative Rebuttal	5 minutes	Second Affirmative Speaker
6. Cross-Examination	3 minutes	First Negative Speaker questions Second Affirmative Speaker answers
7. First Negative Rebuttal	5 minutes	Second Negative Speaker
8. Cross-Examination	3 minutes	First Affirmative Speaker questions Second Negative Speaker answers
9. Final Affirmative Rebuttal	5 minutes	Third Affirmative Speaker
10. Final Negative Rebuttal	5 minutes	Third Negative Speaker

Activity sheets may be downloaded from www.idebate.org/environment.htm.

ENVIRONMENT AND THE LAW—UNDERSTANDING BASIC ENVIRONMENTAL TERMS AND PHRASES

OBJECTIVES

Upon completion of this lesson, students will be able to define a number of terms related to the environment.

BACKGROUND

By becoming familiar with certain basic environmental terminology, students will be better able to understand and discuss contemporary environmental issues and laws.

MATERIALS

Definitions Only sheet (one copy for each group)
Envelopes (one for each group)
Environmental Terms activity sheet (copies for each student)
Glossary Terms and Definitions resource sheet

TEACHER TIPS

This lesson is geared toward students at the upper end of the age group.

ACTIVITY

Preparation

Duplicate Definitions Only sheet so you have one copy for each small group. Cut the sheet along the dotted lines and place the definitions in an envelope.

1. Explain to your students that if they want to understand contemporary environmental issues and help improve the environment they need to understand certain basic environmental terminology.

2. Distribute Environmental Terms activity sheet to each student and ask the class to write definitions for the listed words and phrases. Explain that this is not a test, that you are not even going to look at what they wrote and that it is unlikely that any one person will be familiar with all of the terms listed.

3. Divide the class into groups. Allow the students in each group to discuss their answers among themselves.

4. Give each group an envelope containing the cut-up definitions. Tell them to find the term that fits the definition.

5. Re-assemble the class and review the terms and definitions by allowing individuals from each group to explain the terms. Refer to Glossary Terms and Definitions resource sheet, if necessary.

DEFINITIONS ONLY

Acidic precipitation (acid deposition) caused primarily by the release of sulfur dioxide and nitrogen oxides from the burning of fossil fuels. It occurs not only as wet precipitation (rain, mist, snow) but also as dry particles that are absorbed directly by lakes, plants, and masonry.

An underground rock formation through which large amounts of water can flow.

The buildup of harmful substances (pesticides for example) in the food chain. Each higher level of the food chain accumulates more of the harmful substance than was evident in a lower level of the food chain.

Certain substances that destroy targeted living organisms. They can be natural or manmade. Pesticides are biocides.

That part of the Earth on which and in which life can exist; all living beings together with their environment.

A substance incidentally produced during a manufacture of some other substance.

A product, exposure to which can cause cancer.

The average weather (wind, temperature, precipitation) at any specific place over a number of years.

To make something dangerous or unfit for use by contact or introduction of a harmful substance.

Serious, negative change in landscape caused by (1.) human activity either directly (as in certain mining techniques) or indirectly (as in erosion resulting from some farming practices) or (2.) a natural disaster (for example, a tremendous flood).

The study of the relationship between living things and their physical environment.

A serious negative situation affecting the environment. It may be caused by human society (as in a large oil spill in the sea) or natural forces (for example, an erupting volcano could cause an ecological crisis).

Environmentally responsible thinking based on an understanding of and respect for the natural world and the connection between human beings and the natural world.

An integrated unit consisting of the living organisms and the physical environment in a particular area.

Substances that are released into the environment during manufacturing or treatment processes.

The complete disappearance of a species from the Earth.

The local environment where an animal or plant lives and which provides all its needs.

Dangerous.

A method for disposing of solid waste in which the refuse is spread and compacted and a cover of soil applied to minimize the effects on the environment (including public health and safety).

Water that collects contaminants as it trickles through wastes, pesticides, or fertilizers.

The regular, continuous measuring of an environmental condition (the water in a particular stream, for example) by observing, collecting, and/or analyzing samples.

A bluish gas (O_3) formed naturally in the upper atmosphere that helps to protect the Earth from the harmful effects of ultraviolet radiation from the Sun. Ozone is a severe form of pollution when it is created in the lower atmosphere (low-level ozone).

A part of the atmosphere that is at a height of approximately 19–50 kilometers above the Earth. The ozone layer shields the Earth from harmful ultraviolet rays.

Substances that contaminate the environment.

A group of creatures of the same species that are in sufficiently close contact to enable the different individuals to interbreed.

Parts of the Earth that governments choose to protect through laws. National parks are an example of protected areas.

The wearing away and redistribution of the Earth's soil layer by wind or water.

A substance, usually a liquid, that will dissolve another.

A class of organisms having common attributes that can mate to produce fertile offspring.

Poisonous.

Various substances that result from and remain after human activity and that then enter the environment because people do not, or cannot, reuse or recycle them.

Activity sheets may be downloaded from www.idebate.org/environment.htm.

ENVIRONMENTAL TERMS

ACID RAIN:

AQUIFER:

BIOACCUMULATION:

BIOCIDE:

BIOSPHERE:

BY-PRODUCT:

CARCINOGEN:

CLIMATE:

CONTAMINATE:

DEVASTATION OF LANDSCAPE:

ECOLOGY:

ECOLOGICAL CRISIS:

ECOLOGICAL THINKING:

ECOSYSTEM:

EMISSION, EXHAUST, OR DISCHARGE:

EXTINCTION:

HABITAT:

HAZARDOUS:

LANDFILL:

LEACHATE:

MONITORING:

OZONE:

OZONOSPHERE OR THE OZONE LAYER:

POLLUTION:

POPULATION:

PROTECTED AREAS:

SOIL EROSION:

SOLVENT:

SPECIES:

TOXIC:

WASTE:

Activity sheets may be downloaded from www.idebate.org/environment.htm.

GLOSSARY TERMS AND DEFINITIONS

acid rain Acidic precipitation (acid deposition) caused primarily by the release of sulfur dioxide and nitrogen oxides from the burning of fossil fuels. It occurs not only as wet precipitation (rain, mist, snow) but also as dry particles that are absorbed directly by lakes, plants, and masonry.

aquifer An underground rock formation through which large amounts of water can flow.

bioaccumulation The buildup of harmful substances in the food chain. Each higher level of the food chain accumulates more of the harmful substance than was evident in a lower level of the food chain.

biocide Certain substances that destroy targeted living organisms. They can be natural or manmade. Pesticides are biocides.

biosphere That part of the Earth on which and in which life can exist; all living beings together with their environment.

by-product A substance incidentally produced during a manufacture of some other substance.

carcinogen A product, exposure to which can cause cancer.

climate The average weather (wind, temperature, precipitation) at any specific place over a number of years.

contaminate To make something dangerous or unfit for use by contact or introduction of a harmful substance.

devastation of landscape Serious, negative change in landscape caused by (1.) human activity either directly (as in certain mining techniques) or indirectly (as in erosion resulting from some farming practices) or (2.) A natural disaster (for example, a tremendous flood).

ecology The study of the relationship between living things and their physical environment.

ecological crisis A serious negative situation affecting the environment. It may be caused by human society (as in a large oil spill) or natural forces (for example, an erupting volcano).

ecological thinking Environmentally responsible thinking based on an understanding of and respect for the natural world and the connection between human beings and the natural world.

ecosystem An integrated unit consisting of the living organisms and the physical environment in a particular area.

emission, exhaust, or discharge Substances that are released into the environment during manufacturing or treatment processes.

extinction The complete disappearance of a species from the Earth.

habitat The local environment where an animal or plant lives and which provides all its needs.

hazardous Dangerous.

landfill A method for disposing of solid waste in which the refuse is spread and compacted and a cover of soil applied to minimize the effects on the environment (including public health and safety).

leachate Water that collects contaminants as it trickles through wastes, pesticides, or fertilizers.

monitoring The regular, continuous measuring of an environmental condition (the water in a particular stream, for example) by observing, collecting, and/or analyzing samples.

ozone A bluish gas (O_3) formed naturally in the upper atmosphere that helps to protect the Earth from the harmful effects of ultraviolet radiation from the Sun. Ozone is a severe form of pollution when it is created in the lower atmosphere (low-level ozone).

ozonosphere or the ozone layer A part of the atmosphere that is at a height of approximately 19–50 kilometers above the Earth. The ozone layer shields the Earth from harmful ultraviolet rays.

pollution Substances that contaminate the environment.

population A group of creatures of the same species that are in sufficiently close contact to enable the different individuals to interbreed.

protected areas Parts of the Earth that governments choose to protect through laws. National parks are an example of protected areas.

soil erosion The wearing away and redistribution of the Earth's soil layer by wind or water.

solvent A substance, usually a liquid, that will dissolve another.

species A class of organisms having common attributes that can mate to produce fertile offspring.

toxic Poisonous.

waste Various substances that result from and remain after human activity and that then enter the environment because people do not, or cannot, reuse or recycle them.

ENVIRONMENT AND THE LAW—HUMAN BEHAVIOR AND THE ENVIRONMENT

OBJECTIVES

Upon completing this lesson, students will be able to

1. Better understand the mutual relationship and interdependence between human beings and the natural world,

2. Realize that each part of the environment is very important and that making changes in one part of the environment will affect other parts, and

3. Recognize that working toward the protection of the environment today will improve the quality of life for future generations.

BACKGROUND

Human Behavior and the Environment activity sheet will help to demonstrate how much your students already understand about the environment. It will also help to determine areas for further study. Some questions contained in the test relate to everyday life and are designed to demonstrate the importance of each individual in working to protect the environment.

MATERIALS

Human Behavior and the Environment activity sheet (copies for each student)

TEACHER TIPS

This lesson reinforces the philosophy of the curriculum. Continually reviewing the theme of unity throughout these lessons will strengthen the emphasis on the necessity of community involvement.

ACTIVITY

1. Tell students that this activity will demonstrate how much each of them already knows about the environment. Explain that this test will not be graded.

2. Distribute Human Behavior and the Environment activity sheet and ask the students to complete it to the best of their ability.

3. Divide the class into groups and give the individuals in each group time to discuss their answers with each other.

4. Review correct answers with the entire class and ask students to volunteer examples from their own experiences that relate to the test questions.

HUMAN BEHAVIOR AND THE ENVIRONMENT

1. If your bathtub faucet drips 250 ml (1/4 liter) of water every 10 minutes, and if this amount of water would add up to one full tub of water each week, how much water would be wasted from this one faucet in your home each year?

   (a) 1 bathtub filled with water

   (b) 12 bathtubs filled with water

   (c) 52 bathtubs filled with water

2. If you do not let the water run while brushing your teeth, you can save up to 4 liters of water each time you brush. If you brush your teeth twice daily, you can save up to 8 liters each day. Think about how much water a family of four could save in a year if everyone turned off the water while brushing their teeth. Would it be enough water to:

   (a) fill up the sink

   (b) fill up the bathtub

   (c) provide a day's worth of drinking water to more than 7,000 people

3. Which way does a great amount of heat escape from your home in winter?

   (a) along your telephone line

   (b) through closed windows

   (c) by television

4. Which of the following items contribute the most to forming the hole in the ozone layer? (two answers)

   (a) smoke from chimneys

   (b) propellants used in aerosol sprays

   (c) chemicals used in refrigerators and air conditioners

5. We can reduce erosion by

   (a) planting trees and other plants

   (b) leaving the ground around our homes bare and exposed to the weather

   (c) allowing cattle to graze along the shorelines

6. Planting trees in a town park will

    (a) bring more unwanted insects into the area

    (b) help reduce the harmful effects of air pollution

    (c) create a fire hazard

7. List some of the reasons for reduction of the rain forest in Central America, South America, Asia, and Africa.

8. What are some of the reasons for damage to forested areas in Europe and North America?

9. Explain some ways in which water pollution can occur.

HUMAN BEHAVIOR AND THE ENVIRONMENT

1. If your bathtub faucet drips 250 ml. (1/4 liter) of water every 10 minutes, and if this amount of water would add up to one full tub of water each week, think about how much water would be wasted from this one faucet in your home each year.

   ANSWER: (c) 52 bathtubs filled with water

   (What may initially seem to be only a small amount of wasted water adds up to a great loss of water in the course of a year. If each home in your city or region has even one dripping faucet, imagine the tremendous quantity of water being wasted. Imagine this waste across your entire country and across many countries. It is important for each of us to be responsible regarding water use in our own home.)

2. If you do not let the water flow while brushing your teeth, you can save up to 4 liters of water each time you brush. If you brush your teeth twice daily, you can save up to 8 liters each day. Think about how much water a family of four could save in a year if each member of the family turns off the water while brushing their teeth. It would be enough water to

   ANSWER: (c) provide a day's worth of drinking water to more than 7,000 people

   (Scientists have determined that a human being needs approximately 1.6 liters of water daily to maintain good health. Remember that water is in everything you drink and eat. Think about other ways that you and your family can save water around your home. Think about how valuable that water is to all the inhabitants of the Earth.)

3. Which way does a great amount of heat escape from your home in winter?

   ANSWER: (b) through closed windows

   (In some climates more than half of the energy used in homes is used for heating. Unfortunately, much of that heat can be lost through inefficiency. If we take proper action to reduce this waste, we can save energy that will then be available for other families to heat their homes. What kinds of things can be done to reduce heat loss through windows?)

4. Which of the following items contribute the most to forming the hole in the ozone layer?

   ANSWER: (b) propellants used in aerosol sprays and (c) chemicals used in refrigerators and air conditioners

5. We can reduce erosion by

    ANSWER: (a) planting trees and other plants

6. Planting trees in a town park will

    ANSWER: (b) help reduce the harmful effects of air pollution

7. List some of the reasons for reduction of the rain forest in Central America, South America, Asia, and Africa.

    ANSWER: Reasons for this deforestation include farming, pasturing livestock, cutting wood for lumber, and mining.

8. What are some of the reasons for damage to forested areas in Europe and North America?

    ANSWER: Acid rain and population growth could be listed here as well as the reasons listed in the answer to question 7.

9. Explain some ways in which water pollution can occur.

    ANSWER: Oil spills, discharges from sewage treatment plants, toxic discharges from industry, and garbage being dumped into seas are all examples of sources of water pollution.

Activity sheets may be downloaded from www.idebate.org/environment.htm.

ENVIRONMENT AND THE LAW–ENVIRONMENT, LAW, AND RESPONSIBILITY

OBJECTIVES

Upon completing this lesson, students will be able to

1. Identify laws designed to protect the environment;

2. Understand that laws will not improve anything unless people actively observe them, and unless individuals and businesses are held accountable to these laws; and

3. Realize that the first step necessary to improve the environment is for each of us to improve the ways in which we interact with our own immediate environment.

BACKGROUND

Students should come to recognize that in a democratic society there are usually many laws that deal with environmental protection. But if we are to protect the environment, we must combine legislation with personal responsibility. Every citizen must be responsible for the environment in his or her everyday actions. Each of us can begin at home and at our school or our place of employment. We will automatically improve the environment of our neighborhoods, cities, countries, and the planet when we make these positive changes in our everyday lives. We can also take direct action to improve the environment through participation in cleanup days, letter-writing campaigns, and other environmentally related activities.

MATERIALS

Activity 1: Environmental Laws and Me activity sheet (copies for each student)
Poster board
Ruler
Markers
Activity 2: The Pyramid activity sheet (copies for each student)
Activity 3: None

TEACHER TIPS

For more information about U.S. environmental laws, you can go to the U.S. Environmental Protection Web site at http://www.epa.gov/epahome/laws.htm.

ACTIVITY

ACTIVITY 1: ENVIRONMENTAL LAWS AND ME

1. Distribute Environmental Laws and Me activity sheet. Review each of the laws on the sheet and ask each student to fill in how the law might be violated and what the student could do if it were.

2. Create a master list on the chalkboard using the information from the student activity sheets.

ACTIVITY 2: THE PYRAMID

1. The pyramid provides a way for us to try to visualize the various levels of each person's environment and our environmental responsibility. Draw the following on the chalkboard:

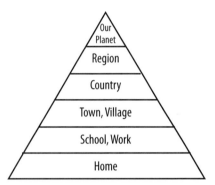

2. Distribute The Pyramid activity sheet. Ask students to complete the right side of the pyramid by listing concrete examples of activities that they could perform to protect or improve the environment at each level.

3. Ask volunteers to make a master pyramid from the class's suggestions and post it on the classroom wall.

ACTIVITY 3: CODE OF LAW

1. Have the class create a "code of law" for environmental protection at the school. Distribute copies of the final code to each student.

2. Arrange for the class to present the code to other classes both to solicit their support and to determine if other students might have valuable suggestions to add to the list.

3. Have your students present their code to the student government and principal, lobbying for its approval.

4. Post the environmental code where everyone in the school will have an opportunity to read it.

ENVIRONMENTAL LAWS AND ME

Law	Possible Violation	How Can I Intervene?
The Clean Air Act (1970) regulates air emissions from area, stationary, and mobile sources.		
The Clean Water Act (1977) establishes the basic structure for regulating discharges of pollutants into U.S. waters.		
Comprehensive Environmental Response, Compensation, and Liability Act (Superfund) (1980) provides broad federal authority to respond directly to releases or threatened releases of hazardous substances that may endanger public health or the environment.		
The Endangered Species Act (1973) provides a program for the conservation of threatened and endangered plants and animals and the habitats in which they are found.		
The Oil Pollution Act (1990) enables the Environmental Protection Agency to take measures to prevent and respond to catastrophic oil spills.		
The Resource Conservation and Recovery Act (1976) gives the Environmental Protection Agency the authority to control the generation, transportation, treatment, storage, and disposal of hazardous waste and manage non-hazardous waste.		
The Safe Drinking Water Act (1974) protects the quality of U.S. drinking water.		
The Toxic Substances Control Act (1976) gives the Environmental Protection Agency the ability to control industrial chemicals as necessary to protect human health and the environment.		

Activity sheets may be downloaded from www.idebate.org/environment.htm.

THE PYRAMID

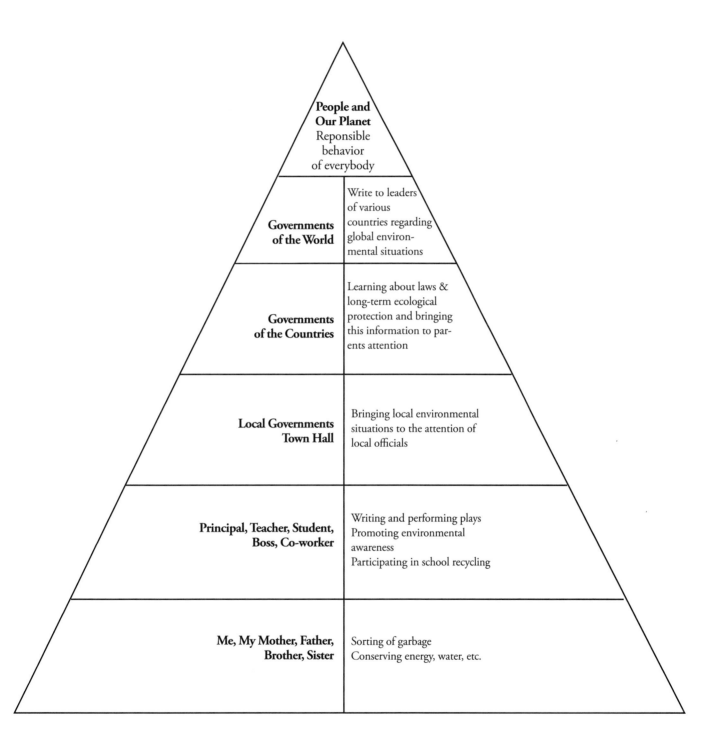

People and Our Planet
Reponsible behavior of everybody

Governments of the World — Write to leaders of various countries regarding global environmental situations

Governments of the Countries — Learning about laws & long-term ecological protection and bringing this information to parents attention

Local Governments Town Hall — Bringing local environmental situations to the attention of local officials

Principal, Teacher, Student, Boss, Co-worker — Writing and performing plays
Promoting environmental awareness
Participating in school recycling

Me, My Mother, Father, Brother, Sister — Sorting of garbage
Conserving energy, water, etc.

THE PYRAMID

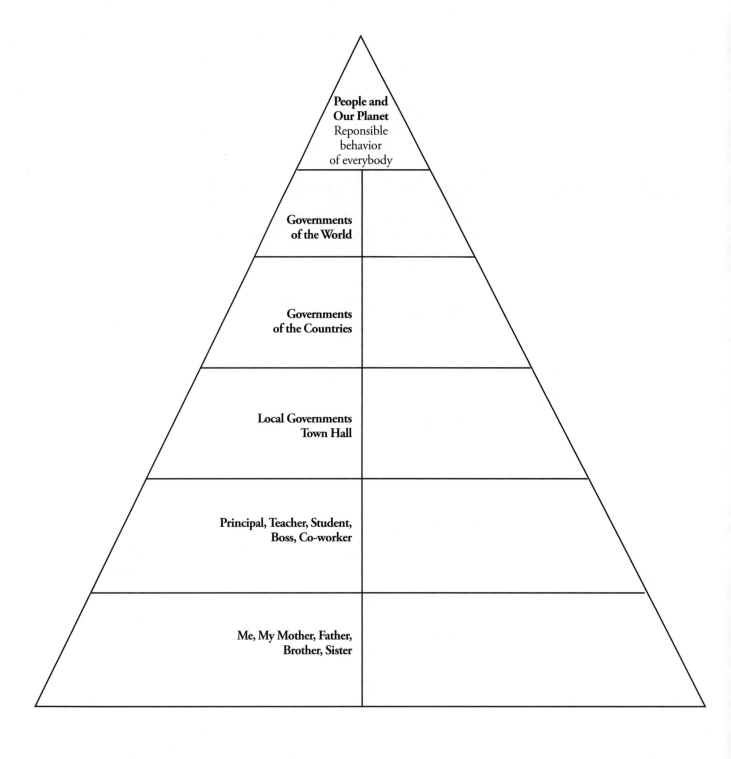

People and Our Planet
Reponsible behavior of everybody

Governments of the World

Governments of the Countries

Local Governments Town Hall

Principal, Teacher, Student, Boss, Co-worker

Me, My Mother, Father, Brother, Sister

Activity sheets may be downloaded from www.idebate.org/environment.htm.

REUSE, RECYCLE, AND MINIMIZE WASTE

OBJECTIVES

Upon completing this lesson, students will be able to

1. Distinguish between items for the home that are necessary and those that are not and

2. Describe the changes they and their families could make in their own home that might have a positive effect on what and how products in the home are used.

BACKGROUND

We live in a "throwaway" society where consumers are encouraged to purchase new, often unnecessary things, and to discard their older things. Most people fail to realize that this lifestyle has an adverse effect on the environment. We use up raw materials to produce things we do not really need and create tremendous waste problems when we throw away old possessions. We should all realize that the environment will be healthier if we own and use fewer products and recycle the possessions we have. This philosophy also makes good economic sense for us as individuals and for our societies.

MATERIALS

Activity 1: Household Products activity sheet (copies for each group)
Newspapers and magazines
Activity 2: Reuse/Recycle activity sheet (copies for each student)

TEACHER TIPS

This activity can be repeated throughout the year. Students may concentrate on their family waste first, then develop a school project, a neighborhood project, and, finally, a community project at the end of the year.

ACTIVITY

ACTIVITY 1: HOUSEHOLD PRODUCTS

Preparation

Gather, or ask the students to gather, magazines and newspapers that contain pictures of houses, rooms, and advertisements for products for the home.

1. Begin by explaining that many articles and products are essential to our lives while others are not. Some that are not may be harmful to the environment, or the way we use or dispose of them may be harmful to the environment.

2. Form the class into small groups and distribute Household Products activity sheet to each group. Give each group several magazines and newspapers and tell them to list all the items for the home they find in the magazines in the appropriate categories on the activity sheet.

3. When the groups have finished, ask the students the following questions:

    + Which list is longest?

    + Why do you think people buy things that they do not need?

    + Why do you think people believe that they need certain things?

    + Why is it sometimes difficult to resist purchasing things that we do not need?

    + What products did you put on the "unnecessary" list and why?

    + How can using different things or using things differently in the home affect the environment?

    + What can you and your family do to be wiser consumers of products for the home?

Activity 2: Reuse/Recycle

1. Explain that when we buy something, we should use it as long as we can. If we can no longer use a product or no longer want it, we should try to find a new use for it or recycle it.

2. Distribute copies of Reuse/Recycle activity sheet and ask the students to complete it, either individually or in small groups.

3. Create a master list from the class's suggestions.

HOUSEHOLD PRODUCTS

Necessary	Satisfy the need for comfort and convenience in some way	Unnecessary

REUSE/RECYCLE

ITEM	Find new use	Turn into different product	Give item to someone who can use it	Recycle
1.				
2.				
3.				
4.				
5.				
6.				
7.				
8.				
9.				
10.				
11.				
12.				
13.				
14.				
15.				
16.				
17.				
18.				
19.				
20.				

UNIT THREE
Learning About Pollution:
Scientific Knowledge to Guide Our Decisions

❦

AIR POLLUTION

OBJECTIVES

Upon completing this lesson, students will be able to

1. Identify several types of air pollution,

2. Describe the causes and effects of some kinds of air pollution, and

3. Recognize some of the steps they can take to prevent air pollution.

BACKGROUND

Because they often cannot see air pollution, students may have difficulty understanding the impact on a personal level. The activities below are designed to show students that they experience the effects of air pollution every day and to help them understand the causes of air pollution.

MATERIALS

Activity 1: Air Pollution Survey activity sheet (copies for each student)
Activity 2: White sock, tape, plastic bag
Activity 3: What's in the Air? activity sheet (see activity sheet for materials needed)
Activity 4: Air Pollution Math activity sheet (copies for each student)
Activity 5: Air Pollution fact sheet (copies for each student)
Air Pollution Sources activity sheet (copies for each student)

TEACHER TIPS

You may have to simplify the fact sheet for younger students. If so, emphasize the importance of fossil fuels in contributing to air pollution and how our modern lifestyle is connected to fossil fuel use.

ACTIVITY

ACTIVITY 1: AIR POLLUTION SURVEY

Distribute Air Pollution Survey activity sheet. Ask the students to walk around the school yard and/or neighborhood and look for sources of air pollution. Re-assemble the class and prepare a master list.

Activity 2: Cars and Pollution

Prepare the sock before the class: secure the white sock to the tailpipe of an automobile. Start the car and run it for a few minutes. After the car engine is turned off, allow the tailpipe to cool and remove the sock. Store the sock in a plastic bag until needed for the activity.

Ask the students to examine the sock you secured to the tailpipe. What does the sock tell them about automobile emissions?

Activity 3: What's in the Air?

Perform the activity What's In the Air? to help students see the air pollution that surrounds them every day.

Activity 4: Air Pollution Math

Ask your students to solve the math problems in Air Pollution Math.

Activity 5: Air Pollution Sources

1. Form the class into pairs and distribute Air Pollution Sources activity sheet and Air Pollution fact sheet. Review the fact sheet.

2. Tell each pair to think of some local sources of air pollution and write them down.

3. Have each pair develop five questions they could ask the class based on the material in Air Pollution fact sheet.

4. Have the pairs present their questions to the entire class and discuss the class's answers. If necessary, assign students to research questions.

5. Compile a master list of local sources of air pollution. Ask the class to brainstorm ways they can reduce this pollution.

AIR POLLUTION SURVEY

SOURCES OF AIR POLLUTION

A. In my school

1. _____
2. _____
3. _____
4. _____
5. _____
6. _____
7. _____
8. _____

B. In my neighborhood

1. _____
2. _____
3. _____
4. _____
5. _____
6. _____
7. _____
8. _____

WHAT'S IN THE AIR?

MATERIALS

two 5 x 7 index cards
two pieces of acetate 2" x 2"
ruler
pen
petroleum jelly

PROCEDURE

1. Decide where you want to place your two air pollution detectors. One location should be inside, the other outside.

2. Draw a half-inch grid on each of the two index cards. Write the location and date on each.

3. Punch two holes in each card and draw the string through to create a handle.

4. Spread a thin layer of petroleum jelly on each card.

5. Press a piece of acetate on each card.

6. Hang the detectors in the appropriate locations. Make sure no one will disturb them.

7. Collect the detectors after several days and examine them. Compare the portion of the card covered with acetate to that left uncovered.

8. Count the particulate matter in four grid squares and use that to calculate the average particulate matter per square.

9. Compare the amount of particles collected indoors and outside.

10. Observe the factors that may have affected the numbers.

AIR POLLUTION MATH

FACTS

+ Driving an automobile 1 kilometer will put 28 kilograms of CO_2 into the atmosphere.

+ The average car uses 1 liter of gasoline to travel 8.08 kilometers.

SOLVE THE FOLLOWING PROBLEMS:

A. How many kilograms of CO_2 will 4 liters of gasoline put into the atmosphere?

B. You live 5 kilometers from school and 2 kilometers from the grocery store. Suppose your family uses an automobile five days a week to transport you to and from school and two days a week to travel to the grocery store.

    + How many kilograms of CO_2 does your family release into the atmosphere each week? Each year?

    + In 10 years?

How might your family reduce the amount of CO_2 it releases into the atmosphere?

Activity sheets may be downloaded from www.idebate.org/environment.htm.

AIR POLLUTION

Every mammal needs to breathe in order to survive. The quality of the air we breathe is very important to our health and longevity. But in many large cities and industrial areas various factors, such as factories and traffic, have combined to cause pollution, which lowers the quality of our air. Usually air pollution will be at its worse on calm, cloudy days because there is little wind to disperse it. If people spend too much time outside on days like these, they may find that their eyes burn or itch, or they may develop a headache, a sore throat, or breathing difficulties.

Sometimes we can see and smell air pollution. Look around your city. Can you see smoke coming out of chimneys? Can you see and smell exhaust coming out of the tailpipes of cars? Do you see the black grime left on your windowsills? Some forms of pollution, however, are invisible. These include carbon monoxide, carbon dioxide, sulfur dioxide, nitrogen oxides, and chlorofluorocarbons.

CAUSES AND EFFECTS OF AIR POLLUTION

One of the greatest causes of air pollution is the burning of fossil fuels. Fossil fuels are composed of non-renewable resources like coal, oil, and some forms of gas. We use them to heat our homes, run industrial plants, and fuel our cars. Until there is a commitment to using alternate sources of energy, the world will continue to be dependent on fossil fuels, and their widespread use will cause significant problems. The incomplete or improper burning of these fuels generates both particulate matter and invisible gases that are harmful to human health and damage the environment.

Particles from incomplete combustion have an effect on both humans and their surroundings. In a heavily polluted area, buildings and statues are covered with a film of oily grime that can eventually damage their surfaces. Humans inhale these particles that are then deposited in the lungs, where they may contribute to disease.

Among the invisible gases generated by the burning of fossil fuels are carbon monoxide, carbon dioxide, sulfur dioxide, and nitrogen oxides. Carbon monoxide (CO) is a colorless, odorless gas that is heavier than air, and so its polluting effects are most noticeable closest to the ground, where people live and breathe, rather than in the upper atmosphere. CO attaches itself to the hemoglobin in your blood, depriving your cells of oxygen. Because the attachment of CO to hemoglobin is more than 200 times stronger than that of oxygen to hemoglobin, carbon monoxide is not expelled from the body in normal breathing. People exposed to CO experience headaches; heavy, labored breathing; fatigue; dizziness; giddiness; and chest pain. In extreme cases, CO can cause unconsciousness and death.

Like CO, nitrogen oxides are also heavier than air and therefore lie close to the ground. Air pollutants like these are especially dangerous to small children because they linger where little children are breathing. In large concentrations, nitrogen oxides and sulfur dioxide can irritate the lining of the eye. These chemicals are transformed into acid in the mucus of the air path, irritating and damaging cells.

When air-polluting chemicals like nitrogen oxides and sulfur dioxide rise into the atmosphere, they can combine with water vapor and return to the Earth in the water cycle as acid rain, which can damage forests, buildings, and water supplies.

GREENHOUSE EFFECT

The burning of fossil fuels also produces carbon dioxide (CO_2). Plants need this chemical for their survival, but too much CO_2 causes an imbalance in the atmosphere that is bad for the environment. Large quantities of CO_2 can trap heat from the Sun on the Earth, causing temperatures to rise. This is called the greenhouse effect. Scientists have warned that global warming can cause severe ecological damage and make human life more difficult.

CHLOROFLUOROCARBONS

Many scientists and environmentalists are also concerned about the hole in the ozone layer in the stratosphere (one of the upper layers of the atmosphere). For many years the chlorofluorocarbons used in refrigeration equipment and air conditioners and as industrial solvents have contributed to this problem. The ozone layer serves as protection for the Earth by filtering out ultraviolet radiation from the Sun. Because of the hole in the ozone layer, more radiation is reaching the Earth's surface, where it may cause increased skin cancers.

Activity sheets may be downloaded from www.idebate.org/environment.htm.

AIR POLLUTION SOURCES

List five sources of air pollution.

1. _____

2. _____

3. _____

4. _____

5. _____

Read air pollution fact sheet and think of five questions you could ask the class based on the information in the sheet.

1. _____

2. _____

3. _____

4. _____

5. _____

As a result of what you have learned about the sources of air pollution, how can you change your life to limit air pollution?

GLOBAL WARMING

OBJECTIVES

Upon completing this lesson students will be able to

1. Understand how their family's lifestyle impacts global warming,

2. Understand how their nation contributes to global warming, and

3. Develop ideas of how to counter global warming.

BACKGROUND

Global climate changes have occurred naturally throughout Earth's history, usually over long periods—sometimes millions of years. But today we may be witnessing a rapid climate change due to the emission of greenhouse gases, including carbon dioxide, that result from industrialization and modern lifestyles revolving around the burning of fossil fuel. The U.S. Environmental Protection Agency estimates that a typical American household of two generates approximately 60,000 pounds (30 tons) of carbon dioxide emissions from household activities and transportation annually. These emissions contribute to global warming, which could raise the surface temperature of the Earth enough to cause ecological damage and make human life more difficult.

MATERIALS

Activity 1: U.S. Household Emissions resource sheet (copies for each student)
My Household Emissions activity sheet (copies for each student)
Activity 2: Possible Results of Global Warming resource sheet (copies for each student)
Possible Impact of Global Warming activity sheet (copies for each student)
Activity 3: Global Carbon Dioxide Emissions resource sheet (copies for each student)
Activity 4: Solving Global Warming activity sheet (copies for each student)

TEACHER TIPS

Activity 1: If the students have access to computers, they can do a more precise calculation by using the Personal GHC Calculator on the EPA Web site: http://yosemite.epa.gov/oar/globalwarming.nsf/content/ResourceCenterToolsGHGCalculator.html.

ACTIVITY

ACTIVITY 1: MY HOUSEHOLD EMISSIONS

1. Distribute U. S. Household Emissions resource sheet and discuss.

2. Distribute My Household Emissions activity sheet. Ask the students to take it home and have their parents help them complete it.

3. Once the individual sheets are completed, have the students calculate the annual CO_2 emissions for the class and for the school.

ACTIVITY 2: POSSIBLE RESULTS OF GLOBAL WARMING

1. Distribute and review Possible Results of Global Warming resource sheet.

2. Distribute Possible Impact of Global Warming activity sheet. Based on your discussion of the resource sheet, ask the students to indicate how each result might affect agriculture, natural ecosystems, and humans.

ACTIVITY 3: GLOBAL EMISSIONS

1. Distribute and review Global Carbon Dioxide Emissions resource sheet.

2. Ask the students to draw pie charts based on the information on the resource sheet.

3. Ask if they were surprised at the percentage their area is contributing and will contribute to CO_2 emissions.

ACTIVITY 4: THINK GLOBALLY, ACT LOCALLY

1. Write the phrase "Think Globally, Act Locally" on the board. Ask the students what they think it means and how this type of thinking might help solve the problem of global warming.

2. Distribute Solving Global Warming activity sheet and ask the students to think of what they and their family, their country (all its people, industry, etc.), and the international community can do to solve the problem of global warming.

3. Have the students share their ideas with the entire class and create a master list of ideas.

U.S. HOUSEHOLD EMISSIONS

The U.S. Environmental Protection Agency estimates that a typical American household of two annually generates approximately 60,000 pounds (30 tons) of carbon dioxide emissions from household activities and transportation.

AVERAGE YEARLY U.S. HOUSEHOLD EMISSIONS (HOUSEHOLD OF 2)	
Source	**Pounds carbon dioxide per year**
Transportation (per car)	13,500
Electricity	20,000
Home heating	
natural gas	11,000
oil	14,500
Waste	4,800

Source: U.S. Environmental Protection Agency, Global Warming Resource Center,
http://yosemite.epa.gov/oar/globalwarming.nsf/content/ResourceCenterToolsGHGCalculator.html.

MY HOUSEHOLD EMISSIONS

INSTRUCTIONS:

Calculate your family's emissions using the chart below. Pick the figures that are closest to your family's usage.

		CO_2 emissions (lbs)	My family's annual CO_2 emissions (lbs)
Transportation			
miles put on car per week? (multiply emissions by number of cars in family)	200	11,804	
	400	23,608	
	600	35,412	
Electricity			
average monthly electric bill	$40	9,840	
	80	19,680	
	120	29,520	
Home Heating			
average monthly natural gas bill	$50	11,116	
	100	22,232	
	200	44,465	
or			
average monthly fuel oil bill	$50	14,530	
	100	29,061	
	200	58,122	
Recycling			
we never recycle		5,700	
we recycle about half of recyclable materials		3,900	
we recycle everything we can		2,100	

Activity sheets may be downloaded from www.idebate.org/environment.htm.

POSSIBLE RESULTS OF GLOBAL WARMING

As a result of global warming, temperatures rise, possibly causing the following:

1. Reduction in sea ice

2. Rise in sea level

3. Changes in the intensity and frequency of tropical storms

4. Deforestation and desertification

5. Drier summers in temperate mid-continental regions

6. Increased global precipitation

7. Changes in regional distribution of precipitation

8. Changes in regional vegetation

9. Dramatic alterations of ecosystems

10. Loss of animal and plant species

POSSIBLE IMPACT OF GLOBAL WARMING

1. Reduction in sea ice

Impact on agriculture:

Impact on ecosystems:

Impact on humans:

2. Rise in sea level

Impact on agriculture:

Impact on ecosystems:

Impact on humans:

3. Changes in the intensity and frequency of tropical storms

Impact on agriculture:

Impact on ecosystems:

Impact on humans:

4. Deforestation and desertification

Impact on agriculture:

Impact on ecosystems:

Impact on humans:

5. Drier summers in temperate mid-continental regions

Impact on agriculture:

Impact on ecosystems:

Impact on humans:

6. Increased global precipitation

Impact on agriculture:

Impact on ecosystems:

Impact on humans:

7. Changes in regional distribution of precipitation

Impact on agriculture:

Impact on ecosystems:

Impact on humans:

8. Changes in regional vegetation

Impact on agriculture:

Impact on ecosystems:

Impact on humans:

9. Dramatic alterations of ecosystems

Impact on agriculture:

Impact on ecosystems:

Impact on humans:

10. Loss of animal and plant species

Impact on agriculture:

Impact on ecosystems:

Impact on humans:

Activity sheets may be downloaded from www.idebate.org/environment.htm.

GLOBAL CARBON DIOXIDE EMISSIONS

CO_2 EMISSIONS (1998)

Area	Percent
Africa	4
Canada	2
Central and South America	4
China	12
Developing Asia	12
Eastern Europe	3
Former Soviet Union	10
Japan and Australia	6
Mexico	2
Middle East	4
United States	25
Western Europe	16

Source: U.S. Environmental Protection Agency, http://yosemite.epa.gov/oar/globalwarming.nsf/content/EmissionsInternationalInventory.html.

PROJECTED CO_2 EMISSIONS (2020)

Area	Percent
Developing World and China	50
United States	21
Organization for Economic Cooperation and Development, Europe, and Asia	18
Former Soviet Union and Eastern Europe	11

Source: Adapted from U.S. Environmental Protection Agency,
http://yosemite.epa.gov/oar/globalwarming.nsf/content/EmissionsInternationalProjections.html.

Activity sheets may be downloaded from www.idebate.org/environment.htm.

SOLVING GLOBAL WARMING

1. Steps My Family and I Can Take to Solve the Problem of Global Warming

2. Steps My Country Can Take to Solve the Problem of Global Warming

3. Steps the International Community Can Take to Solve the Problem of Global Warming

INDOOR AIR POLLUTION

OBJECTIVES

Upon completing this lesson students will be able to

1. Identify major sources of indoor air pollution and

2. Understand how they can eliminate or minimize these sources.

BACKGROUND

When we think of air pollution, we usually think of the gases and particulate matter released into the air outside our homes. But our homes also contain sources of pollution. Building materials, some consumer products, gas appliances, and cigarettes can give off toxic gases or particles that can harm human health. Short-term exposure can result in eye and throat irritation; long-term can lead to respiratory disease and cancer. Exposure to high levels of some pollutants, such as carbon monoxide, can even result in immediate death. As a result of research, federal scientists have ranked indoor air pollution as one of the most important environmental problems in the United States.

MATERIALS

Sources and Potential Health Effects of Indoor Air Pollutants resource sheet (copies for each student)

Indoor Pollution activity sheet (copies for each student)

TEACHER TIPS

Make sure the students know the definitions of the pollutants listed in the table.

ACTIVITY

1. Distribute Sources and Potential Health Effects of Indoor Air Pollutants resource sheet and discuss.

2. Distribute Indoor Pollution activity sheet and ask the students to think of ways they can eliminate or minimize indoor pollution.

3. Once they have completed the activity sheets, have the students share the suggestions with the entire class.

4. Make a master sheet of suggestions. Use the master sheet to create a brochure the students can take home to their parents.

SOURCES AND POTENTIAL HEALTH EFFECTS OF INDOOR AIR POLLUTANTS

INDOOR POLLUTANTS		
Pollutant	**Major Indoor Sources**	**Potential Health Effects***
Tobacco Smoke	Cigarettes, cigars, and pipes	Respiratory irritation, bronchitis and pneumonia in children, emphysema, lung cancer, and heart disease
Carbon Monoxide	Unvented or malfunctioning gas appliances, wood stoves, and tobacco smoke	Headache, nausea, angina, impaired vision and mental functioning, fatal at high concentrations
Nitrogen Oxides	Unvented or malfunctioning gas appliances	Eye, nose, and throat irritation; increased respiratory infections in children
Organic Chemicals	Aerosol sprays, solvents, glues, cleaning agents, pesticides, paints, moth repellents, air fresheners, dry-cleaned clothing, and treated water	Eye, nose, and throat irritation; headaches; loss of coordination; damage to liver, kidney and brain; various types of cancer
Formaldehyde	Pressed wood products such as plywood and particle board; furnishings; wallpaper; durable press fabrics	Eye, nose, and throat irritation; headache; allergic reactions; cancer
Particulates	Cigarettes, wood stoves, fireplaces, aerosol sprays, and house dust	Eye, nose, and throat irritation; increased susceptibility to respiratory infections and bronchitis; lung cancer
Biological Agents (Bacteria, Viruses, Fungi, Animal Dander, Mites)	House dust; pets; bedding; poorly maintained air conditioners, humidifiers, and dehumidifiers; wet or moist structures; furnishings	Allergic reactions; asthma; eye, nose, and throat irritation; fever, influenza, and other infectious diseases
Asbestos	Damaged or deteriorating insulation, fireproofing, and acoustical materials	Asbestosis, lung cancer, mesothelioma, and other cancers

Pollutant	Major Indoor Sources	Potential Health Effects*
Lead	Sanding or open-flame burning of lead paint; house dust	Nerve and brain damage, particularly in children; anemia; kidney damage; growth retardation
Radon	Soil under buildings, some earth-derived construction materials, and groundwater	Lung cancer

* Depends on factors such as the amount of pollutant inhaled, the duration of exposure, and susceptibility of the individual exposed.

Source: California Air Resources Board, http://www.arb.ca.gov/research/indoor/rediap.htm.

INDOOR POLLUTION

Pollutant	What My Family and I Can Do
Tobacco Smoke	
Carbon Monoxide	
Nitrogen Oxides	
Organic Chemicals	
Formaldehyde	
Particulates	
Biological Agents	
Asbestos	
Lead	
Radon	

Suggestions for eliminating and minimizing pollutants

Use products safely.
Restrict smoking.
Use appliances properly.
Select building materials and furniture properly.
Practice good housekeeping.
Provide adequate ventilation.

Activity sheets may be downloaded from www.idebate.org/environment.htm.

NOISE POLLUTION

OBJECTIVES

Upon completing this lesson, students will begin to understand the need to regulate noise in their own environment.

BACKGROUND

Noise can reduce the quality of life and negatively impact people's health. Loud sounds can generate physiological changes in the body that are associated with stress-related disorders such as

- high blood pressure
- coronary disease
- ulcers
- colitis
- migraine headaches

Noise interferes with communication and performance and disturbs sleep. Extremely loud noise can even result in hearing loss. In 1991 the U.S. Public Health Service reported that almost half of the people with hearing impairments suffered hearing loss due to noise pollution. In this activity, students will learn how everyday activities contribute to noise pollution.

MATERIALS

Activity 1: Noise at Home activity sheet (copies for each student)
Activity 2: Recording of various sounds, some of which are soothing and others of which would create noise pollution
Activity 3: Noise Levels activity sheet (copies for each student)

TEACHER TIPS

Ask the students to compare the volume of the music they listen to with the volume of music their parents and grandparents listen to.

ACTIVITY

ACTIVITY 1: NOISE AT HOME

1. Distribute Noise at Home activity sheet and ask the students to complete the first column as homework.

2. Organize the class into small groups and have the students discuss their lists. Ask them to determine which sounds were pleasant and which might contribute to noise pollution.

2. Re-assemble the class and make a master list of the sounds that might contribute to noise pollution.

3. Consider the following questions with your class:

   + How does loud noise affect you, your parents, your grandparents?

   + Do you and your parents have a different tolerance for noise? Explain how you differ from your parents.

   + Do you think the government should institute regulations limiting noise? What types of regulations would you suggest?

   + What sounds do you like? In your home, your school, your community?

   + What sounds do you dislike? In your home, your school, your community?

   + When does noise begin to disturb you?

   + If there is noise pollution in your life, is there anything that you can do to reduce it?

ACTIVITY 2: IDENTIFYING SOUNDS

Preparation

Recording of various sounds, some of which are soothing and others of which would create noise pollution.

Play the audiotape you made. Ask the students to guess what some of the sounds on the tape are, where various portions of the tape were made, and if some of the sounds contribute to noise pollution.

ACTIVITY 3: NOISE LEVELS

1. Distribute Noise Levels activity sheet and discuss how loud noise is harmful to health.

2. Ask the students to record on the sheet how many times they hear the specific noises.

3. Ask them to use the findings from their sheet to write a paragraph about noise in their lives.

NOISE AT HOME

INSTRUCTIONS:

Sit down in your living room. Close your eyes for 30 seconds and really listen intently. Open your eyes and quickly list the sounds that you heard. Repeat this process in each room of your home. Bring the lists to school but do not discuss them or show them to your classmates until instructed to do so.

Pollutant	Pleasant	Contributes to Noise Pollution
Living Room		
Dining Room		
Kitchen		
Bedroom		
Bathroom		
Other		

NOISE LEVELS

Noise levels above 85 decibels will harm hearing over time. Noise levels above 140 decibels can cause damage to hearing after just one exposure

POINTS OF REFERENCE	
0	the softest sound a person can hear with normal hearing
10	normal breathing
20	whispering at 5 feet
30	soft whisper
50	rainfall
60	normal conversation
110	shouting in ear
120	thunder

Review the list below and indicate in the last column how often you hear the noise.

Noise	Decibel level	How Often I Hear the Noise Frequently / Occasionally / Never
ambulance siren	120	
auto stereo	125	
band concert	120	
bicycle horn	143	
boom box	100	
busy video arcade	110	
car horn	110	
disco	110	
electric drill	95	
firecracker	150	
food processor or blender	80–90	
garbage disposal	70–95	
hair dryer	60–95	

Noise	Decibel level	How Often I Hear the Noise Frequently / Occasionally / Never
heavy traffic	85	
jackhammer, power drill	130	
leaf blower	110	
motorcycle	95–110	
noisy restaurant	85	
noisy squeeze toys	135	
personal cassette player on high	112	
power lawn mower	65–95	
power saw	110	
public safety siren	130	
rock concert	110–120	
school dance	100	
shouted conversation	90	
snow blower	105	
snowmobile	100	
stock car races	130	
subway	90–115	
truck	90	
vacuum cleaner	60–85	

Source: League for the Hard of Hearing, http://www.lhh.org/noise/decibel.htm.

ACID RAIN

OBJECTIVES

Upon completing this lesson, students will be able to

1. Describe the formation of acid rain;

2. Understand the ways acid rain hurts human health, food crops, aquatic life, bodies of water, monuments, buildings, and forests; and

3. Develop ideas about how they and their society can deal with the problem.

BACKGROUND

Acid rain is a serious environmental problem that affects large parts of the world. It damages forests and soils, fish and other living things, buildings and cultural monuments, and human health. In this activity, students will learn how acid rain develops and study its effects through research and experimentation.

MATERIALS

Acid Rain fact sheet (copies for each student) (optional)
Activity 1: Acid Rain activity sheet (copies for each student)
Activity 2: Pictures of things affected by acid rain (building, animal, statue, old piece of metal pipe, insect, fish, tree or forest, person, lake or stream, field or farm crop, etc.)
Activity 3: Illustrating Acid Rain activity sheet (see activity sheet for materials needed)

TEACHER TIPS

You may want to use Acid Rain fact sheet to give your students general background on the topic.

Activity 2: Depending on the size of the class, you can use separate pictures for each student, or you can duplicate pictures so that students can work in pairs or small groups.

ACTIVITY

ACTIVITY 1: DIAGRAMMING ACID RAIN

Distribute Acid Rain activity sheet. Ask students to read the paragraph describing the formation of acid rain and then draw a picture or diagram illustrating the process.

ACTIVITY 2: EFFECTS OF ACID RAIN

Preparation

Hide the pictures around the classroom before the students enter.

1. Ask the students to search for pictures you have placed around the room. Once they have found a picture, ask them to take it and return to their seats. They are to take only one picture.

2. Tell the students that they are to research the effects of acid rain on the object in the picture and ask them to present arguments for and against laws to control acid rain. Ask them to also present ways in which they could change their lifestyle to help prevent acid rain. If the students are working in pairs or in small groups, have them meet to coordinate their research.

3. Have the students or groups present their findings to the class.

ACTIVITY 3: EXPERIMENTS ILLUSTRATING ACID RAIN

Perform the experiments in Illustrating Acid Rain activity sheet to see the impact of acid rain on buildings and plants.

ACID RAIN

Acid rain, what scientists call acid deposition, forms when certain chemicals are absorbed into the atmosphere and then fall to the Earth as precipitation or as gases and particles. The primary source of acid rain is the burning of fossil fuels in industry, power plants, and motor vehicles. These fuels produce sulfur dioxide, nitrogen oxides, and other pollutants. The lighter particles of these pollutants are swept into the upper atmosphere, where they react with ozone and other compounds to form sulfuric and nitric acids. These acids return to Earth in rain, fog, and snow, damaging food crops, fish and aquatic life, forests, buildings, and human health.

About half of the acidity in the atmosphere falls back to Earth as acidic particles and gases that damage buildings, cars, homes, and trees. Rainstorms can also wash these dry deposits into the water supply, which may already be affected by acid rain, making the water even more acidic.

Prevailing winds blow the compounds that cause acid deposition across state and national borders, and sometimes over hundreds of miles.

Using the information above, draw a diagram or picture of the acid rain cycle.

Activity sheets may be downloaded from www.idebate.org/environment.htm.

ILLUSTRATING ACID RAIN

EXPERIMENT 1

MATERIALS

two bowls
vinegar
tap water
piece of chalk

PROCEDURE

Place a piece of chalk in a bowl with white vinegar. Place another piece in a bowl of tap water. Leave the dishes overnight. The next day, see if the students can tell which piece of chalk is more worn away. (This experiment enables students to see the effect of acid rain on marble and limestone because chalk is made of calcium carbonate, a compound occurring in rocks such as these.)

EXPERIMENT 2

MATERIALS

two clear glasses
tap water
vinegar
two plant cuttings

PROCEDURE

Fill one glass with tap water and one with a mixture of nine parts water and one part vinegar. Place a cutting of a plant in each glass and put the plants by a sunny window. Have the students observe root growth after a week.

Activity sheets may be downloaded from www.idebate.org/environment.htm.

ACID RAIN

The Water Cycle is a continuously revolving process. When the Sun heats the water in streams, lakes, oceans, and other aquatic bodies, some of it rises from the Earth's surface in a vapor. As the water vapor climbs into the atmosphere, it expands and cools because of the low pressure at high altitudes. At this stage, the water vapor forms into small droplets that can be seen as clouds. If the water droplets continue to cool, they can combine to form larger drops. Because of their increased weight, these larger drops will fall to the Earth as rain, sleet, or snow. Some of this water will sink into the Earth, and some will be absorbed by plants, but the rest will enter into streams, lakes, oceans, and other bodies of water, where it will begin to evaporate and re-start the Water Cycle.

Exhaust from industry, transportation, and the burning of fossil fuels produces pollutants that circulate in the air. Sources of exhaust include automobiles, factories, and power plants. These are easy to identify because of the dark smoke that funnels out of exhaust pipes or smoke stacks. Some of these pollutant gases are sulfur dioxide, hydrocarbons, and nitrogen oxides.

Some of the sulfur dioxide and nitrogen oxides in our atmosphere are produced by natural sources such as volcanoes, biological decay, and forest fires. The rest are human-made and are therefore concentrated near or downwind from cities and towns. The heavier particles of these pollutants will fall back to the Earth, but the lighter particles are swept into the upper atmosphere with the clouds. These upper atmospheric pollutants may be blown far distances away, or may react with water droplets in the clouds and fall with rain near the source of the pollution. When the pollutants react with the water droplets, they form very dilute acids: sulfuric acid and nitric oxide. This acid rain, no matter how dilute, damages food crops, fish and aquatic life, forests, buildings, and human health.

Acid rain can be especially harmful if it collects in snow. As snow piles up on the ground during the winter, the acidity gradually increases; the top layers of snow melt, leaving acidic pollutants behind in the bottom layers. As more snow falls and melts away, the bottom layers become increasingly acidic. Therefore, when the snow completely melts, there is an immediate "acid shock" that can kill many plants and animals.

There are two primary dangerous effects from acid rain. First, the acidic nature of the rain alone can be harmful. Secondly, the acid rain can react with rocks in the ground to cause an overload of minerals in the soil.

Food crops are believed to be damaged by the increased acidity and mineral concentration of the soil caused by acid rain. Lettuce, oats, and wheat are especially affected. A great reduction in the amount of these crops can be seen in areas heavily affected by acid rain. This damage also results in harmful effects on human health. Because of the imbalance of minerals in soil, plants can have high concentrations of certain harmful minerals in them. Humans are affected when they eat these plants or eat animals that have been feeding on these plants.

Humans are also hurt by drinking water that contains acid rain. Rain flows into lakes and streams that are used as sources for drinking water. If the rain is acidic, the water used for drinking will also be acidic. The acidic pollutants in the water can react with water pipes, causing metals to be dissolved into our drinking water.

Stone buildings, statues, and monuments are also hurt by acid rain. The acids in the rain react with the stonework, especially marble, limestone, and sandstone, to release part of it as gas, while some of the stonework simply crumbles away.

Acid rain damages forests by disrupting the acidic level and mineral concentration of the soil. This damages the roots of the trees, making them more susceptible to other factors that can kill them. Forests are not only valued for their beauty and for recreation but are also necessary for our ecosystem, as habitats for many species, and for the production of oxygen.

Acid rain can also hurt many forms of aquatic life. Aquatic life can be killed not only by the change in the acidity and mineral concentration in the water that acid rain produces but also by the breaking of the food chain. Therefore, although acid rain may initially kill only a lake's insect or plant life, the fish will also die because they have no insects to feed on. The result is "dead" lakes that contain no living plants, insects, or animals. We must be especially concerned over the loss of food and recreation that aquatic life provides.

We can do a lot to reduce the amount of acid rain-forming pollutants released into the air. If we use less electricity, less fossil fuel will have to be burned to produce electricity. This can be accomplished by using better home insulation to reduce the electricity needed for cooling and heating and by using more energy efficient machines. Factories can reduce the amount of sulfur they emit into the atmosphere by using fuel that is low in sulfur and by removing sulfur either during combustion or before the smoke is released. Sulfur dioxides, hydrocarbons, and nitrogen oxides can also be reduced by developing cars that burn gas more efficiently and by lowering speed limits. Such measures will reduce incomplete combustion and therefore lessen the amount of these pollutants.

Groups concerned about acid rain have had considerable success in convincing their governments to pass laws designed to reduce the problem. One way they have accomplished this is by writing letters to their government leaders asking for strong laws aimed at curbing factory and power plant emissions and making cars more fuel efficient.

WATER POLLUTION

OBJECTIVES

Upon completing this lesson, students will be able to

1. Describe the sources of water pollution and how they affect water quality,

2. Identify ways to change their lifestyles to limit water pollution, and

3. Understand how difficult it can be to remove pollutants from water.

BACKGROUND

Water pollution is a broad term that encompasses a number of threats to the Earth's water. It can be caused by natural processes such as erosion, volcanic activity, and the decay of organic matter, or by human activities. Chemical spills, toxic runoff, and untreated wastes all contribute to pollution. Students frequently assume that industries, power plants, and agriculture are the sources of water pollution, but in these lessons they learn that their lifestyle also contributes to the problem. Finally, they learn how difficult it can be to treat water pollution.

MATERIALS

Water Pollution fact sheet (copies for each student) (optional)
Activity 1: Water Pollution summary sheet (copies for each student)
Activity 2: Geological map of your area, or map showing lakes, rivers, streams, etc.
Activity 3: Household Contaminant Survey activity sheet (copies for each student)
Activity 4: Cleaning Dirty Water activity sheet (see activity sheet for materials needed)

TEACHER TIPS

You may want to distribute Water Pollution fact sheet to give your students general background on the topic. If you are working with younger students, you may need to simplify the summary sheet.

ACTIVITY

ACTIVITY 1: SOURCES AND EFFECTS OF POLLUTION

Distribute Water Pollution summary sheet and review. Ask the students to draw a picture or diagram illustrating how various types of pollutants get into the water and how they affect water quality.

ACTIVITY 2: LOCAL SOURCES OF POLLUTION

Have your students look at a map of your area to determine all of the water sources that are located nearby. Investigate possible sources of pollution located on or near these sources.

ACTIVITY 3: HOUSEHOLD CONTAMINANTS

1. Distribute Household Contaminant Survey. Ask the students to survey their homes and gardens and make a list of products that would be dangerous to the environment if they were dumped down the drain.

2. Ask them to research the proper way to dispose of each and suggest an environmentally friendly alternative.

3. Once the surveys are completed, compile a master list. Duplicate and distribute so that students can share it with their families.

ACTIVITY 4: CLEANING DIRTY WATER

Perform the experiment Cleaning Dirty Water to demonstrate to students the difficulty in removing pollutants from water.

WATER POLLUTION

Type of Pollution	Source	Impact
Biodegradable wastes	• Human waste • Animal waste • Food scraps and other organic material	• Provides nutrients for bacteria that consume enough oxygen so that everything else in the water dies • Spreads disease-causing bacteria such as those causing typhoid fever and cholera
Chemical pollution	• Improperly treated industrial discharge • Toxic runoff from roads and highways • Pesticides used in farming • Accidents such as oil spills • Household chemicals	• Endangers aquatic life • Over the long term, accumulates in living organisms, which, when eaten, can cause serious health problems in humans
Excessive sediment	• Construction • Poor farming techniques • Livestock operations • Logging • Flooding • Runoff from city streets, parking lots, and buildings	• Transports heavy metals and other contaminants • Clogs and fills in lakes • Smothers aquatic life • Clouds water and prevents photosynthesis, endangering plant life • Reduces level of oxygen, endangering aquatic life • Creates thermal pollution
Heat	• Power plants • Industrial equipment	• Reduces the diversity of species needed for the health of a stream

Type of Pollution	Source	Impact
Plant nutrients	• Sewage and septic runoff • Livestock waste • Fertilizer runoff • Detergents • Industrial wastes	• Stimulates algae growth that chocks off other life forms • Causes eutrophication, which impairs water quality • Produces hydrogen sulfide gas, which smells like rotten eggs • Releases toxins that concentrate in fish, causing human digestive problems
Radioactive waste	• Factories • Hospitals • Uranium mines	• Accumulates in the body, where it can cause cancer and death

Source: U.S. Environmental Protection Agency, *The Water Sourcebooks*, http://www.epa.gov/safewater/kids/wsb/pdfs/FACTS.pdf.

HOUSEHOLD CONTAMINANT SURVEY

1. Survey your home and garden and list any products that would be dangerous to the environment if they were dumped down the drain.

2. Research the proper way to dispose of each and indicate in the second column.

3. Use the third column to suggest environmentally friendly products.

CONTAMINANT SURVEY		
Product Name	**Disposal Procedure**	**Environmentally Friendly Alternative**

CLEANING DIRTY WATER

MATERIALS

clear drinking water

Per group: three glasses
                     cooking oil
                     spoons
                     cotton balls
                     cloth
                     coffee filters
                     food strainers
                     food basters
                     food coloring
                     dirt
                     sponges
                     absorbent powder (e.g., cornstarch)
                     household cleaning supplies (e.g., soap, dish detergent, laundry detergent, etc.)

PROCEDURE

1. Divide the class into groups. Give each group three glasses that are 3/4 full with water.

2. Explain to your students that each group operates a wastewater treatment facility. One company that sends wastewater to their facility uses oil. This oil becomes mixed with their wastewater. Have each of your groups pour some cooking oil into one glass of water to simulate wastewater coming from this facility.

3. Tell your students that there is also a chemical plant located in their treatment area. Have each of the groups pour some food coloring into a second glass of water to simulate a chemical spill at the plant. This chemical spill has contaminated water that will now come to their facility for treatment. Explain that in this case we are lucky because we can see the chemical in the water but with some chemicals this is not the case.

4. The third glass represents water that comes from your students' homes. Have them add a little soap and dish or laundry detergent to the water. Have them add a significant amount of dirt to the water to simulate the septage coming out of their houses.

5. Pass out spoons, cotton balls, small pieces of cloth, coffee filters, food strainers, sponges, absorbent powder, food basters, and any other devices you can locate that students could use to try to remove the "pollution" from their water samples. Also give them extra glasses so that they can pour water from one glass to another while attempting to filter it.

6. Allow about 10 or 15 minutes for this activity. After the allotted time, ask each group to describe their water treatment results.

Activity sheets may be downloaded from www.idebate.org/environment.htm.

WATER POLLUTION

THE WATER CYCLE

Water is constantly being recycled through the Earth and its atmosphere. Much happens to water during this journey, including evaporation, condensation, precipitation, and collection. Most precipitation collects in the oceans and other bodies of water, but a portion of it sinks into the Earth, in a process called percolation, and seeps into the groundwater supply. It returns to the Earth's surface again in springs or wells and travels through bodies of plants, animals, and people. This process, known as the Water Cycle, will continue as long as life, as we know it, exists.

SOURCES AND EFFECTS OF WATER POLLUTION

Some chemical pollutants originate from natural (geological) processes, mainly from the weathering of rocks. However, the great majority of poisonous substances are produced by people. These can be divided into two main categories:

1. Substances that are in themselves poisonous to aquatic life and that also, for a varying amount of time, make water unfit for human consumption. Even when these pollutants are present in small quantities, aquatic organisms often concentrate them in their bodies at rates well above the average concentration in the water.

2. Materials that, although not harmful in and of themselves, alter the normal condition of water, making it difficult for animal and plant life to survive.

Loose soil that is carried into and eventually settles onto the bottom of bodies of water by rain, wind, etc. is called sediment. Although soil is not a human-made material or a pollutant, it can act as a pollutant when too much of it enters bodies of water. When human beings use poor land management practices, excessive amounts of sediment can enter lakes, streams, etc. through soil erosion. This soil can reduce water's capacity to sustain life. Sediment can cloud water, thus reducing light penetration and, in turn, photosynthesis. Soil particles can also be carriers of pollutants. Nutrients, organic matter, and potentially hazardous chemicals can attach to sediment particles and then be transported to surface waters. Luckily, we can reduce the amount of sediment causing water pollution by using better land management practices that do not leave soil bare and vulnerable to the elements and that do not erode shorelines.

Nutrients, such as nitrogen and phosphorus, are essential for aquatic plant growth. But excessive amounts of these nutrients can enter waterways from human activities, such as the use of chemical fertilizers and detergents containing phosphates, animal waste produced on farms, and lack of proper sewage treatment. Nitrogen and phosphorus are now so abundant in our waterways that they are causing one of the most common water pollution problems on the Earth: eutrophication.

The enrichment of lakes, and to a lesser extent streams, by plant nutrients is called eutrophication. Over a long period of time most lakes become choked with algae or weeds. (This is a natural aging process of lakes, but its acceleration by human activities is harmful to aquatic life.) When weeds die and decompose, they consume oxygen in the water.

Plant debris and animal wastes also contribute nutrients and oxygen-demanding materials to our waters. Bacteria decompose organic materials and consume oxygen in the process. If the supply of organic materials is excessive, the oxygen supply may become seriously depleted. Severe oxygen shortages may result in fish kills.

The development of better land management practices will help to limit the amounts of nitrogen and phosphorus entering waterways. Since farms are a major source of these pollutants, many farmers in the United States are now working to reduce their fertilizer and pesticide use.

When speaking about water pollution people often picture a pipe discharging obnoxious looking wastes into a body of water. The origin of pollutants entering water sources ranges from those that are predominantly point sources, like this pipe scenario, to those that are mainly diffuse. In the case of direct discharge of contaminants into our streams and lakes, you can point to the source of the water pollutants involved. That is why these sources of water pollution are referred to as point pollution sources. Some of the more important point sources of water pollution are discharges from sewage treatment plants, industry, and mine drainage. Because it is generally not difficult to locate the source of point pollution, it can be relatively easy to collect and then treat it.

Non-point, or diffuse, sources of pollution can't be traced to specific offenders because they are made up of sources such as agricultural and urban runoff and acid deposition, and because they can include large areas. Sediment, plant nutrients, toxic materials, and animal wastes are the major diffuse source pollutants. These are more difficult to locate and therefore more difficult to control and to treat than pollutants from point sources.

Note that pollutants can interact in complex ways with their surroundings, such as bonding with sediments and releasing additional toxic chemicals.

We can divide different concentrations of pollutants into four categories; pollutants that are found in:

1. water

2. organisms and suspended organic material

3. sediment

4. surface film

The dominant amount of pollutants is located in sediments. In connection with great movements of water in shallow areas such as during spring floods, these pollutants are partly transported into the bulk of water together with the sediments. There is also horizontal transport within lakes, rivers, and seas.

Ocean Pollution

Sea and ocean pollution is an important environmental concern. It was not long ago that seas were regarded by many people as nature's garbage can. All sorts of wastes were dumped into the sea. By now, ocean currents have distributed the negative results of this ocean dumping over wide areas to many countries. In some countries beaches have had to close because of high levels of bacteria in the water, or the garbage that has washed up onto the shore. This garbage is not just unattractive, it is dangerous to human health and to the health of marine life.

It is not simply municipal waste that has been dumped into the sea. Governments of various countries have disposed of military waste, including extremely hazardous chemical and nuclear wastes, in this way. It is good news for all of us that much of this type of disposal of hazardous and military waste is now prohibited. However, we must face the fact that some governments may not voluntarily comply with international laws and that accidents (such as those involving nuclear submarines) can occur, and we must also address pollution problems caused by past ocean disposal. This is an area where governments of many countries can work together to solve the environmental problems of the past for the benefit of everyone on the planet.

Scientists have determined that about 3/4 of all the pollution entering our oceans is being produced on land by human beings. Pollution can travel great distances in our waterways, so that, even if you do not live in a coastal area, the wastes that you produce and that are produced by the industries, farms, and sewage plants in your town can end up in our oceans. Much of the air pollution that human beings produce also settles into the oceans. By living in an environmentally responsible way, each of us can help to protect our oceans even if we live very far away from them.

Although most of the pollution of our oceans by human beings originates on land, people also contribute to ocean pollution during their use of this tremendous resource. Ships pollute the ocean in several ways. Perhaps the first image that comes to mind is that of a ship flushing human waste into the sea. Many large ships must take on great quantities of water (sometimes many thousands of tons) to maintain stability. This water, and all of the life contained in it, is later released into other parts of the ocean, causing what is sometimes called genetic pollution.

Genetic pollution refers to the introduction of species of plants and animals to an area in which they are not traditionally found. Some species can also be transported to new locations on the hulls of ships. Genetic pollution has caused serious problems in many areas by upsetting the natural balance of the marine environment. Some species have even journeyed beyond coastal areas far up rivers. Some of these introduced species compete with natural species for food or begin using the same species as fishermen for their own food source. Others, such as zebra mussels, which have been introduced into the coastal waters of the United States, have caused problems in industrial settings by attaching to water intake and outlet valves, such as those of nuclear power plants. Genetic pollution can also introduce parasites into new areas.

Laws Protecting Water

Water pollution is a topic that illustrates how, in all societies, one individual's actions may adversely affect many people, and, conversely, how one person's actions (to protect against water pollution and/or against the wasting of water) may benefit many people.

Traditionally, as societies become more industrialized, water pollution becomes more severe. River water quality, for example, can be extremely negatively affected by industrialization. Because rivers don't stop at the borders of countries, industrialization and poor land use practices in one country can affect water quality in other countries and in our oceans. Today many countries are trying to enact laws to prohibit the actions of some individuals and communities that would negatively impact on water used by other communities.

Industries themselves must monitor and control their emissions and take measures toward improvement. With the use of modern technologies, some industrial process waters can now have closed circuits, so that they have no negative ecological effects.

In each individual country there are governing authorities who have the responsibility and power to create and enforce laws governing the prevention of and control of pollution. You can find out about the environmental laws of your country, including those laws governing water pollution, by contacting your national government's officials or your local department of environment protection or similar institution.

Wastewater Treatment

In an effort to combat water pollution, many communities have designed and built wastewater treatment facilities. When individuals living in these communities use water in their homes, businesses, and industries, the water that is left over after use is referred to as wastewater. In poorly developed areas without modern technology wastewater often re-enters the environment untreated. In more technologically advanced areas, wastewater is transported via plumbing to treatment facilities. The goal of these facilities is to remove pollutants from wastewater before releasing the water back into the environment.

Water pollution problems vary from one place to another. For this reason, different wastewater treatment plants must employ different process stages to treat water. Some of the stages of water treatment include pre-cleaning (with mechanical filters), oil separation, neutralization, sedimentation, denitrification, aeration and re-aeration of sludge, biological purification, and final clarification. Unfortunately, at the present time, wastewater treatment facilities cannot combat and/or remove all of the various kinds of pollution found in wastewater. That is one reason why it is important for each of us to be careful about what we put into water as we use it in our daily lives.

Water Quality

Because water is one of the essentials of human life, people are naturally concerned when there appears to be a threat to its quality. On a global scale, thousands of chemicals are used by people on a daily basis. Every time any individual chooses to use a chemical, there is a risk that some of this chemical will end up in water. It is the responsibility of each individual to realize this and to use chemicals only when necessary and then to use them wisely and safely. Fortunately, some chemicals are rapidly transformed and degraded, thereby losing their toxicity. On the other hand, chemically stable or persistent substances can remain in the environment for long periods of time. For example, heavy metals will never be transformed. Some chemicals are able to penetrate biological membranes. Thus, they can be absorbed by bacteria, plants, animals, and people. Such chemicals are said to be bio-available. The most hazardous pollutants are those that are both easily absorbed by various organisms and that last in water for a very long time.

Adverse human health effects can sometimes be linked clearly to specific pollution incidents or environmental accidents. It is more difficult to establish causal links between health effects and generally poor environmental quality, particularly in the case of long-term low-level contamination. This is an important area for research.

Tests to Determine Water Quality

Water quality is a combination of all of its physical, chemical, and biological characteristics. There are several scientific tests that form the basis of analytical investigation of water samples:

pH value: pH is a measure of acidity or alkalinity of water. The pH scale goes from 0 to 14. A pH reading of between 5 and 9 may not cause a negative environmental situation to develop in a stream. However, before being dispensed to the community, water that is used as a drinking supply should have its pH adjusted to between 6 and 8 to avoid the danger of corrosion to plumbing. A pH reading of 7 is neutral.

Conductivity: Conductivity is a measure of water quality that is related to the water's concentration of dissolved salts. Although the absolute measurement of conductivity is of limited value, if the scientist monitoring water notices a sudden change in conductivity, that could indicate a change in dissolved solids content that may be caused by the onset of a polluting discharge into the body of water being monitored.

Biochemical Oxygen Demand: This test gives a measure of the amount of organic matter present. It is dependent on the activities of organisms as small as bacteria and is therefore subject to considerable variation.

Free Ammonia (as Nitrogen): The presence of an appreciable quantity (more than 0.2 ppm, or parts per million) in water offers strong evidence of pollution, since ammonia in general arises as a product excreted by animals.

Nitrite and Nitrate: The ammonia present in sewage is oxidized in the sewage effluent (wastewater) treatment process to nitrite and then to nitrate, so well purified effluent will usually contain a fairly high concentration of total oxidized nitrogen and a low concentration of free ammonia.

Chloride: Chloride is unaltered by the sewage treatment process and its concentration in the sewage effluent can be of value in giving a rough indication of condition of the incoming sewage.

Dissolved Oxygen: The dissolved oxygen measurement is basic to studies of organism distribution, respiration, and production in aquatic systems. It is an indication of the suitability of water for most life forms. It is also dependent on temperature of the water, time of day, sunlight, and other factors.

A study of the organisms living in water can also supply much information concerning rivers, lakes, and other bodies of water. Whereas a chemical analysis shows the quality of water at the time that the sample tested was taken, studies of the organisms living in water can give a better indication of the usual condition of the water. Animals in the water are present all of the time and act as nature's own monitoring system. This is because different groups of aquatic animals express different tolerances to pollution and thrive best under a narrow range of conditions.

YOU AND WATER POLLUTION

Water pollution is a problem we associate mainly with industry and agriculture. But we are all capable of producing water pollution in our own homes. Therefore, we are also capable of preventing water pollution.

Does your family use environmentally friendly cleaning products? Cleaning fluids, such as bleach, are harmful to the environment. There are now alternative cleaners for bathrooms and toilets that are made from natural substances. These substances can be broken down by bacteria without causing damage to the environment. You can use toilet paper that is made from recycled paper and that has not been bleached with chlorine. It is important to remember the environment when shopping and to shop wisely and responsibly.

Many garden fertilizers have the same effects as phosphates when they get into a body of water. Pesticides—poisonous chemicals that are sprayed on gardens to kill pests—can do much environmental damage when rain washes them into water. If you must use fertilizers and pesticides, look for products that will not harm the environment. You can use natural fertilizers and pesticides that break down naturally in the environment. You can also use your consumer power to encourage organic farming practices and the manufacture of environmentally friendly products. Everyone's voice counts in the marketplace.

REMEMBER: Environmentally friendly products are biodegradable, phosphate free, contain no unnecessary perfumes and ingredients, and have been tested to measure their environmental impact. A golden rule to follow with ALL products is to use LESS of them. This way your family can really help to protect the environment.

DRINKING WATER

OBJECTIVES

Upon completing this lesson, students will be able to

1. Understand how scarce drinking water is,

3. Describe how various contaminants can pollute drinking water, and

5. Understand the mechanisms used to clean drinking water and wastewater.

BACKGROUND

Earth is often called the "water planet" because of its abundant water—in the oceans, in the atmosphere, in glaciers, and as freshwater on land. Water covers 75 percent of the surface of the Earth yet less than half of 1 percent of this water is available for people's use. This precious supply of freshwater is increasingly vulnerable to human abuse and threatened by eutrophication, heavy metals, persistent organic pollutants, acidification, and sewage pollution. The following activity helps students understand how scarce usable water is, how it is purified for human use, and how wastewater is treated to protect the environment.

MATERIALS

Activity I: World's Water resource sheet (copies for each student)
Earth's Water activity sheet (copies for each student; see activity sheet for materials needed)
Activity 2: Water Pollution fact sheet (from previous lesson) optional
Water Treatment resource sheet (copies for each student)
Activity 3: Building a Simple Treatment System activity sheet (copies for each student; see activity sheet for materials needed)

TEACHER TIPS

Rather than have the class do the activity in Earth's Water activity sheet, you may want to ask older students to suggest a way of illustrating the information on World's Water resource sheet.

ACTIVITY

ACTIVITY 1: THE WORLD'S WATER SUPPLY

1. Distribute World's Water resource sheet and discuss.

2. Use Earth's Water activity sheet to show students how little of Earth's water is available for human use.

ACTIVITY 2: WATER TREATMENT SYSTEMS

1. Review the types of water pollution (from the previous lesson). If necessary, consult Water Pollution fact sheet.

2. Have the class research which groups of pollutants are the most common in local water, where these pollutants originate, and what harms they cause to the environment.

3. Explain that water that enters municipal water supplies must be purified before and after it is used. Distribute Water Treatment resource sheet and discuss.

4. Ask the students to draw diagrams illustrating the purification and waste treatment processes.

ACTIVITY 3: BUILDING A SIMPLE TREATMENT SYSTEM

You can use Building a Simple Treatment System activity sheet to have your students construct a simple filtration system.

WORLD'S WATER

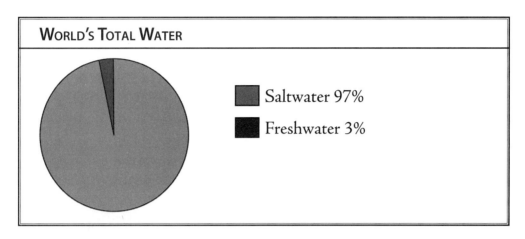

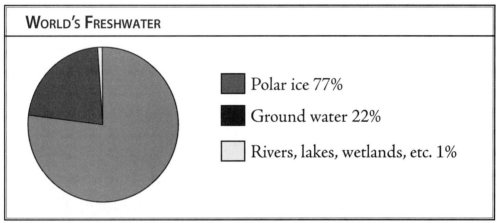

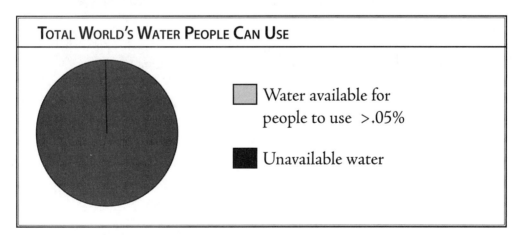

Source: U.S. Geological Survey. Water Science for Schools, http://ga.water.usgs.gov/edu/earthhowmuch.html

EARTH'S WATER

MATERIALS

three cups freshwater
four clear plastic cups
teaspoon and 1/8 teaspoon measuring spoons
red and blue food coloring
marker

PROCEDURE

1. Label the cups as follows:

> Cup 1: All the World's Water
> Cup 2: World's Saltwater
> Cup 3: World's Freshwater
> Cup 4: Freshwater for People

2. Place 100 teaspoons of water into cup 1.

3. Place 100 teaspoons of water into cup 2.

4. Remove three teaspoons of water from cup 2 and place them in cup 3. Place a few drops of red food coloring in cup 2 and a few drops of blue food coloring in cup 3.

5. Remove 1/8 teaspoon of water from cup 3 and place it in cup 4. This is slightly more than the portion of the world's water available for human use.

Activity sheets may be downloaded from www.idebate.org/environment.htm.

WATER TREATMENT

WATER PURIFICATION PROCESS	
1. Screening	Removes large objects
2. Pre-chlorination	Adds chlorine to kill disease-causing organisms
3. Flocculation	Adds alum and lime to remove suspended particles
4. Settling	Particles and solids allowed to settle to the bottom
5. Sand filtration	Removes nearly all suspended matter
6. Post-chlorination	Chlorine adjusted to maintain long-term action to kill disease-causing organisms
7. Other treatments	Optional treatments, including adjust pH, add fluorine, etc.

WASTEWATER TREATMENT SYSTEM	
1. Screening	Large objects removed; smaller objects ground down; sand and dirt allowed to settle
2. Primary settling	Grease and scum skimmed; solids settle out
3. Aeration	Aeration tanks add air and allow bacteria to digest organic substances
4. Final settling	Sludge is settled, aerated, chlorinated, and dried for incineration or for dumping in landfills
5. Disinfection/chlorination	Chlorine added to kill disease-causing organisms; other disinfection processes such as ultraviolet irradiation may also be used
6. Optional treatments	PH adjusted; heavy metal and phosphate ions removed by precipitation

Source: U.S. Environmental Protection Agency, *The Water Source Books*, http://www.epa.gov/OGWDW/kids/wsb/pdfs/682.pdf.

BUILDING A SIMPLE TREATMENT SYSTEM

MATERIALS

two 10-liter buckets
pipe
plastic net
fine sand
sand
upper layer of soil
muddy water
glass

PROCEDURE

1. Take one 10-liter bucket and insert pipe (with fine plastic net covering one end) at the bottom. Put in the following layers of material (bottom to top):

   > fine sand (1/3 of bucket)
   > sand (1/3 of bucket)
   > upper layer of soil from the nearest farm (1/3 of bucket)

2. Fill the second bucket with very muddy water. Put some of this water in a glass and set it aside.

3. Begin to pour the remaining muddy water slowly on the top layer of the bucket containing the layers of soil until water comes out of the pipe at the bottom. Collect some of this water in a second glass.

4. Compare the visibility of the water coming out with the muddy original water.

5. Draw conclusions about water quality after this experiment is completed.

Activity sheets may be downloaded from www.idebate.org/environment.htm.

ECOSYSTEMS

OBJECTIVES

Upon completing this lesson, students will be able to

1. Understand the concept of an ecosystem and

2. Describe how the various elements of ecosystems interact.

BACKGROUND

An ecosystem is a collection of organisms that function together and with the environment in which they live. It is a series of intricately linked and interdependent parts that make up a complex whole. Ecosystems include both living (animals, plants) and nonliving elements (air, water, rocks, and energy), and they can include human factors—agriculture, houses, cars, industry, etc.—as well. Each factor interacts with and changes the others. In this lesson, students learn about the dynamic qualities of ecosystems and develop ecosystems of their own.

MATERIALS

Activity 1: Natural Ecosystems resource sheet (copies for each student)
Activity 2: Terrarium or aquarium
Materials will depend on what the students want to include in their terrariums or aquariums.

TEACHER TIPS

The aquariums and terrariums you set up can be as complex as the students want, but emphasize that they must take care of them if they are to be successful.

ACTIVITY

ACTIVITY 1: NATURAL ECOSYSTEMS

1. Distribute Natural Ecosystems resource sheet and review.

2. Ask the students to select an ecosystem. It may be the plot of land they investigated in Discovering Nature (page 13), a park or forest they know, or an ecosystem they want to research.

3. Ask them to list the various elements of their ecosystem. They may use Natural Ecosystems resource sheet as reference. They should be as accurate as possible about the names of the plants and animals they put in various categories.

ACTIVITY 2: CREATING AN ECOSYSTEM

1. Tell the students that they will be setting up an ecosystem—a terrarium or aquarium. But they have to plan it carefully for it to be successful.

2. Ask them to use Natural Ecosystems resource sheet to plan what they must include.

NATURAL ECOSYSTEMS

An ecosystem is an integrated unit consisting of the living organisms and the physical environment in a particular area.

Each system is made up of both living and non-living elements. Among the non-living elements are the following:

- sunlight (energy)
- water
- soil (specifically the nutrients—minerals—in the soil)
- air

The living elements include the following:

- plants
- animals
- microorganisms
- fungi

These living things can be put into one of three categories:

- producers
- consumers
- decomposers

These living elements interact as shown in the diagram below.

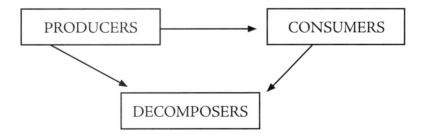

Activity sheets may be downloaded from www.idebate.org/environment.htm.

SHORELINE ECOSYSTEMS

OBJECTIVES

Upon completing this lesson, students will be able to

1. Understand the diversity of species inhabiting shorelines,

2. Know how to make observations about the ecological situation of a shoreline, and

3. Discuss and understand conditions that may cause water pollution.

BACKGROUND

Shoreline ecosystems generally contain a high density of life, and both flora and fauna are usually more diverse in shallow water than in deeper water. Because shorelines and coasts are natural places where human activities meet with aquatic ecosystems, they are excellent places to study the impact of humans on the natural environment and to witness ecological problems firsthand.

MATERIALS

Shoreline Observation Checklist (copies for each student)
Shoreline Ecosystems activity sheet (copies for each student)
Field guide containing pictures of plants and animals likely to inhabit the shorelines in your location
Rubber gloves
Strainer or dip net
Collecting dish (white rectangular baking dish) or large glass jar with lid
Magnifying glass
Spoon
Methyl blue

TEACHER TIPS

Before beginning this activity, consult with government officials to determine if there are any laws governing the collection of plants or animals from local waters.

IMPORTANT! Remember to tell your students to use caution near water. Because this is a lesson on shorelines, it is not necessary for your students to venture into the water. Many rivers and the coasts of large bodies of water have dangerous currents. Even small lakes and ponds may become exceptionally deep very quickly, so watch all of your students very carefully and keep the group close together. Remind them not to drink the water and to wash their hands thoroughly after the activity.

ACTIVITY

This class activity is conducted on the shore of a small pond, lake, or river. For comparative purposes, you may wish to conduct this activity both in a natural area and in an area with human activity present.

1. Before going to the site, review the sources of water pollution from the previous lessons.

2. Remind the students that they must be respectful of nature and disturb the environment as little as possible. Distribute Shoreline Observation Checklist. They may work with a partner, in groups, or as a class to complete the questions.

3. Tell students to put on the rubber gloves (to protect themselves and avoid contaminating the water). Place about 1 inch of water in the collecting dish.

4. Ask the students to stand near the shore and sift water and sediment through the strainer into the collecting jar.

5. Using the magnifying glass and field guide, have the students identify the plants and animals in the sample and record them on Shoreline Observation Checklist. Use the spoon and eyedropper to return the materials to the water.

6. Repeat steps 2 and 3 several times.

7. Tell the students to survey the shoreline and complete Part II of Shoreline Observation Checklist.

8. Ask the students whether there are any signs of pollution near the shore and have them complete Part III of Shoreline Observation Checklist.

9. Explain that organic substances from sewage and wastewater treatment plants can enter water basins. Methyl blue is an indicator of organic activity; the blue color changes to white in the presence of organic substances. Tell the students to place a sample of water in the collection dish and add a few drops of methyl blue. Is there a reaction?

10. Explain that not all organic activity is a result of pollution; it can also be due to natural processes. Ask the students if they think that the activity in their areas is natural or manmade.

11. When the students are back in the classroom, ask them to complete Shoreline Ecosystems activity sheet.

SHORELINE OBSERVATION CHECKLIST

PART I: SHORE WATER SPECIES

Species	Number

PART II: SHORELINE SURVEY

1. Can you see or hear birds nearby? Are there any other signs of bird activity?

2. What other signs of animal life are on the shoreline?

3. Is the area forested?

4. What types of plants are growing near the water?

PART III: POLLUTION SURVEY

1. What is the color of the water? (Pale-colored foam indicates organic activity that may be the result of pollution.)

2. Is the water _____clear _____muddy _____foamy? (Muddy water may be an indication of sediments that could contain pollutants. Excessive sedimentation can also endanger aquatic life by preventing photosynthesis and reducing the levels of oxygen.)

3. What does the water smell like? Is the smell natural (from the decaying of plants and animals)? (An unnatural smell may indicate the presence of pollutants.)

4. In general terms, the greater the varieties of species, the cleaner the water. Judging from the number of animals and plants captured and the diversity of species, is the habitat of the water in healthy or poor condition?

5. Is this an area secluded from or frequented by people? How can you tell?

6. Is there household litter near the shoreline?

7. Is there any evidence of agricultural runoff? How can you tell?

SHORELINE ECOSYSTEMS

FACTORS THAT INFLUENCE THE ECOSYSTEMS OF COASTAL AREAS AND SHORELINES

Name the area(s) you were investigating:

What evidence of pollution did you discover near the water?

List five ways to prevent this pollution:

1.

2.

3.

4.

5.

Write one goal you would want to accomplish to reduce the pollution if you had the power to do something:

Write one goal for improving the ecosystem of this area that you believe you do have the power to accomplish:

PROTECTING ENDANGERED SPECIES

OBJECTIVES

Upon completing this lesson, students will be able to

1. Define the term *endangered species,*

2. Explain why some species of animals and plants are in danger,

3. Understand why human beings should aim to protect all species of animals and plants, and

4. Describe ways that each individual can act to save wildlife.

BACKGROUND

It is very difficult for students to understand why certain species are endangered, because they do not encounter them or their habitats firsthand. This activity shows the students how habitat change can cause an increase or decrease of species in their own neighborhood.

MATERIALS

Endangered Species fact sheet (copies for all students) (optional)
Species in My Neighborhood activity sheet (copies for all students)
Species Form (copies for each species in the project)

TEACHER TIPS

You may want to use Endangered Species fact sheet to give your students general background on the topic.

Learn what you can about plants and animals in your community before you do this activity.

ACTIVITY

1. Introduce the activity by asking the students to define endangered species and leading a discussion about why they think certain species become endangered.

2. Distribute Species in My Neighborhood activity sheet. Ask students to brainstorm the names of plants and animals that live in or near their community. As they name them, list them on the board and tell the students to write them on the activity sheet.

3. Tell the students to take the list home and talk to family members, especially grandparents or older neighbors, about what other species exist, or existed, in or near their community and record that information on the activity sheet. Ask them to discuss with their family and neighbors why some species may have lived there and no longer do, and how long it has been since the species existed in or near the community. They might also ask if the people to whom they talk consider that species to have been important to the community.

4. Within a reasonable time, perhaps one week, ask the students to share their lists with the class. Make a master list of what the students have found and lead a discussion of why certain species are thriving while others have disappeared.

5. From the information that is gathered, students can create a book on neighborhood species for your community. Ask the students to form small groups. Assign each group a portion of the class list of species. Ask each group to continue gathering as much of the following information as possible about each species:

      *   Description

      *   Picture

      *   Habitat

      *   Status

      *   Threats

      *   Actions the community can take to protect the species

      and complete a Species Form for each.

6. Once the information is compiled, the students can produce their book. Ask them what they want to do with it. For example, they might want to put their book in the school library or make presentations to other classes to share what they have learned.

SPECIES IN MY NEIGHBORHOOD

INSTRUCTIONS:

1. List the species that live or lived in your neighborhood. Remember species includes both plants and animals, including insects, birds, and fish.

2. Indicate whether the species has increased, decreased, or disappeared.

3. Explain why.

Species	Status			Why
	Increased	Decreased	Dissapeared	

SPECIES FORM

Species Name:_____

Description: _____
_____
_____
_____

Habitat: _____
_____
_____
_____

Status: _____Increasing   _____Decreasing   _____Disappeared

Reasons for status: _____
_____
_____

Threats to species: _____
_____
_____

Actions the community can take to protect the species: _____
_____
_____
_____
_____

ENDANGERED SPECIES

INTERDEPENDENCE IN ECOSYSTEMS

People sometimes assume that plants and wild animals are free to choose the places where they want to live and that they can choose to settle anywhere. This kind of naive thinking is very dangerous to wildlife. For example, suppose that it is necessary to build a new road connecting two cities. The governments of the areas involved and the designers of the road may simply look at a map and decide where to put the road so that it will cover the shortest distance. Now imagine that the road, if built in this place, will go through a large wetland (marsh or swampy area) where many ducks nest and raise their young. The wetland will have to be filled in to build the road. The government representatives and road builders think that this project will not cause the ducks a problem because only five miles from this wetland there is a very large lake. They think that the ducks can just fly over to the lake and raise their young there. Unfortunately, this is not true. The lake is a different type of habitat than the wetland. The ducks are absolutely dependent on the wetland habitat. If the road is built, the ducks will no longer have a home. It is not just the ducks that will be negatively affected. Every plant, insect, amphibian, mammal, and bird that is a part of the wetland ecosystem will be affected. This is why it is necessary to look very closely at the environmental impact of everything that we plan to do before we do it. Unfortunately, this has not always been done in the past. Now many citizens are insisting that their local government agencies perform environmental impact assessments before starting development activities such as road building.

PLANT-AND-ANIMAL COMMUNITIES

If we look very carefully at the natural world surrounding us, we notice that animal communities are connected with certain plant communities. Good examples of this dependence are the panda, which is almost totally dependent on bamboo for its food supply, and the koala, which is almost totally dependent on eucalyptus. This is what is meant when we speak about plant-and-animal communities. In the same way, plants and animals are associated with certain communities of microbes. Scientists use the word biocenology to describe the study of natural communities and the interaction of the members of these various communities.

The word ecosystem is used to describe certain types of habitat and the communities of plants, animals, and microbes that are suited to, living in, interacting with, and influencing each other in that habitat.

The many different food chains that develop in plant-and-animal communities in various ecosystems are extremely important. In any given ecosystem, certain types of plants provide a food source for certain types of herbivores (plant-eating animals). These animals may in turn supply the food source for certain types of carnivores (meat-eating animals). Some of the animals and plants found in the ecosystem may be providing a food source for omnivores (animals that eat both plants and animals).

Every member is important to the other members and to the ecosystem as a whole. Imagine for a moment that one species of either plant or animal disappears from the ecosystem. The food chain is immediately disrupted and the other members of the association may or may not survive depending upon how essential that one particular element of the food chain was to the survival of the other members of the association.

We can look on a continent as a very large community consisting of smaller communities and ecosystems. Forests, meadows, and wetlands are examples of ecosystems that we might find on our continent. We can also discuss ecosystems and/or communities that are artificial in the sense that they are created and controlled by human beings. A garden, a pasture, and an aquarium are all examples of manmade ecosystems. There are an enormous number of ecosystems and communities covering our planet. Think of the tremendous numbers of species of plants and animals inhabiting those various ecosystems and communities!

SPECIES STATUS

Plants and animals are not spread equally across the planet and they are not equally recognized. Some species are not even known to scientific specialists. For example, many areas in tropical rain forests and in the deepest parts of our oceans have never been studied by human beings. It is very likely that there are species existing in ecosystems like these that have yet to be discovered.

Some species are so rare that they are known only to specialists. There are also well-known plants, animals, reptiles, amphibians, and birds that are now decreasing in number. These decreasing species are sometimes described as threatened species. Finally, there are those species that are in real danger of disappearing forever from the planet. They are called endangered species. Threatened species and, most importantly, endangered species are in need of the assistance of human beings if they are to survive.

WHY SHOULD HUMAN BEINGS PROTECT ENDANGERED SPECIES?

Often we fail to remember that humans are also members of an ecosystem. They too can be affected when a particular species vanishes. For example, many modern medicines have had their origin in the natural world. In some ways the natural world is like a giant pharmacy filled with items yet to be studied. If we allow even one plant to become extinct, it may be that we will have lost the key that one plant held to a cure to some dreaded human disease.

In many traditional cultures, plants and animals have cultural significance for human beings sharing that same ecosystem. In songs, fables, and spiritual beliefs, people affirm the emotional importance of their link to the world of nature. We may value certain species because they are beautiful, or entertaining, or interesting to study, or because they teach us things about ourselves.

WHY ARE SOME SPECIES IN DANGER?

Some species are disappearing because of natural causes. Natural extinction has always been a part of the evolutionary process. Few plants or animals have ever lived longer than several million years without evolving to meet changing circumstances. Sometimes species are not capable of meeting changing climate conditions, or they cannot compete successfully with other species for a food source. In some instances they are too specific in their needs and habits to continue to survive in changing conditions. In other words, human beings are not responsible for all extinction. As in the past, there will always be some species that will, naturally, become extinct. The danger comes when that process is initiated or accelerated by human activity.

For many centuries, people have been altering the surface of the Earth. This leads to changes, some subtle and some drastic, in ecosystems. Human activities have caused the disappearance of many natural dwelling places for plants and animals. Think of the many large cities in the world such as Moscow, New York, Beijing, and others. What types of wildlife once inhabited these areas? What happened to these plants and animals?

Other human activities have had a negative impact on wildlife. Many animal species have decreased or even vanished entirely as a result of hunting. People kill animals for food, clothing, souvenirs, or scientific or pseudo-scientific purposes. Sometimes animals have been exterminated by hunting because some people decided they were undesirable. Now in many areas scientists and others are working to restore animals to places that they once naturally inhabited. For example, there is now an effort underway in the United States to reintroduce the gray wolf to Yellowstone National Park.

HOW CAN WE SAVE WILDLIFE?

One of the first steps in answering this question has been for scientists to try to gather as much information as possible on rare, declining, and endangered plants and animals. Many countries have developed laws aimed at working with scientists to determine which species are endangered, to protect these endangered species, and to assist in the recovery of their numbers.

Like other environmental factors, wildlife has no national boundaries. Thus, it is quite natural that scientists from all over the world are trying to unite in their efforts to protect vanishing and endangered species. One of the main things that people can do to save endangered wildlife is to try to preserve various types of habitats. Many groups have joined together to change laws or to earn money to purchase land areas that are set aside for wildlife, in nature preserves.

PESTICIDES AND THE FOOD CHAIN

OBJECTIVES

Upon completing this lesson, students will be able to

1. Understand what pesticides are and what they are used for,

2. Realize that pesticides influence our environment and recognize some ways that we can reduce the use of harmful pesticides, and

3. Understand and describe how pesticides can circulate and spread through the environment.

MATERIALS

Pesticides resource sheet (copies for each student)
Bioaccumulation activity sheet (copies for each student)

TEACHER TIPS

Bioaccumulation Part II is appropriate for older students.

ACTIVITY

1. Distribute and review Pesticides resource sheet, making sure the students understand how pesticides enter the food chain.

2. Distribute Bioaccumulation activity sheet and ask the students to complete the questions in Part I of the activity sheet. Have them discuss their answers with the class.

3. Ask the students to complete Part II of the sheet, calculating the percentage increase of pesticides up the food chain and creating a bar graph showing the concentration of pesticides in each animal.

PESTICIDES

TYPES OF PESTICIDES	
Type	**Use**
Insecticide	Kills insects
Fungicide	Kills fungi
Bactericide	Kills bacteria
Herbicide	Annihilates weed growth and kills other unwanted plants
Rodenticide	Kills rodents

EFFECTS OF PESTICIDES

Positive

+ Controls agricultural pests, increasing crop yields significantly
+ Controls household pests

Negative

+ destroys valuable insect pollinators
+ leads to development of pesticide resistance organisms
+ increases toxicity of water
+ results in poor tasting water
+ indirectly reduces amount of oxygen in water, affecting aquatic life
+ changes the chemical characteristics of water, affecting aquatic life
+ enters and accumulates in the food chain

BIOACCUMULATION

When transferring from water, soil, and air into the links of the biological chain (food chains), the concentration of pesticides can grow higher by hundreds and thousands of times. For example, plankton organisms are very common, passive floating or weakly swimming animal and plant life found in bodies of water. If plankton are exposed to and begin to accumulate pesticides, these pesticides will then enter into and begin to accumulate in fish, since fish eat the plankton. Every time a fish eats the contaminated plankton, more and more pesticides will enter into its body. Soon the fish will contain more pesticides than any of the individual plankton. Then, if a penguin eats many of these contaminated fish, the penguin will become more and more contaminated with the pesticides. Soon the penguin will contain a higher percentage of pesticides than were in the individual fish.

WAYS PESTICIDES ENTER THE FOOD CHAIN

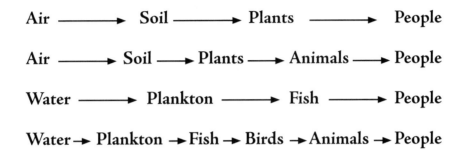

Air ——→ Soil ——→ Plants ——→ People

Air ——→ Soil ——→ Plants ——→ Animals ——→ People

Water ——→ Plankton ——→ Fish ——→ People

Water ——→ Plankton ——→ Fish ——→ Birds ——→ Animals ——→ People

Bioaccumulation

Bioaccumulation					
Animal	Mass of animal (grams)	Number of contaminated animals eaten	Mass of contaminated animals eaten (grams)	Increase in concentration of pollutants (percent)	Concentration of pollutants in the animal (parts per million)
Zooplankton	0.1	---	---	---	0.50
Small fish (2 lbs)	907	100,000	10,000	11.03	5.51
Humboldt penguin (10 lbs)	4,530	8,760	7,945,320	1753.93	318.16

Part I:

Answer the following questions.

1. Which animal will be most affected by the pesticides?

2. What do you think will happen in a longer food chain? If the food chain contained leopard seals, which feed on penguins, and killer whales, which feed on seals.

3. How do you think the pesticides get into the zooplankton?

Part II:

1. Using the information above, calculate the percentage increase of pesticides up an Antarctic food chain.

2. Create a bar chart showing the concentration of pesticides in each animal.

THE ROLE OF THE FOREST AND DEFORESTATION

OBJECTIVES

Upon completing this lesson, students will be able to

1. Define the functions of the forest and how the forest affects human life,

2. Identify causes of deforestation,

3 Understand the negative effects of deforestation,

4. Estimate the usefulness of the forest, and

5. Define their own role and the role of human society in protecting the forest and preventing deforestation.

BACKGROUND

The forest is one of Earth's most productive ecosystems. For many years people looked at it only in terms of its economic value of its timber. Now people are beginning to realize that forests should be valued for their other functions. Forests are producers of abundant and pure soil and water; are habitats for flora and fauna; and are tourist attractions that provide entertainment and cultural inspiration. They also help to establish and preserve the equilibrium of the atmosphere. These ecological functions carry a greater weight than the value of the forest products that result from its exploitation and destruction. In this lesson, the students will learn the importance of forests and investigate the factors that threaten them.

MATERIALS

Activity 1: The Forest Now and After 50 Years activity sheet (copies for each student)
Activity 2: Benefits of One Tree activity sheet (copies for each student)
Activity 3: Deforestation Puzzle activity sheet (copies for each student)
Activity 4: Forest Function and Value resource sheet (copies for each student)
Factors in Deforestation resource sheet (copies for each student)
Photos of a variety of forest conditions such as virgin forest, burning forest, and forest destroyed as a result of various factors

TEACHER TIPS

This lesson identifies the causes of deforestation and the need for trees on our planet. Here is an excellent opportunity to emphasize a POSITIVE APPROACH by planting seedlings and understanding the usefulness of the forest. Activities 1 and 3 are for the younger members of the age group.

ACTIVITY

ACTIVITY 1: FUTURE FORESTS

Have your students define the factors involved in deforestation by completing The Forest Now and After 50 Years activity sheet.

ACTIVITY 2: BENEFITS OF ONE TREE

Have your students complete the math problem in Benefits of One Tree activity sheet.

ACTIVITY 3: DEFORESTATION

Have your students complete Deforestation Puzzle activity sheet and then define some repercussions of deforestation, using answers from the puzzle to help them.

ACTIVITY 4: FOREST FUNCTION AND VALUE

1. Show photos of a variety of forest conditions such as ecosystems of a virgin forest, burning forest, and forests destroyed as a result of various factors such as cutting, acid rain, diseases, insects, and animals. Compare these ecosystems and write down the differences existing between them. Explain the consequences deriving from the deforestation of these places for the air, soil and living world.

2. Distribute and review Forest Function and Value and Factors in Deforestation fact sheets. Ask the students to use the sheets to create a flowchart illustrating the effects of deforestation. Remind them that they must think beyond the effects it has on the natural habitat.

THE FOREST NOW AND AFTER 50 YEARS

Here is a picture of a forest now and how it will look after 50 years. In the clouds above the deforested site are the factors that have brought about the deforestation of this place. Unscramble the words to see what these factors are

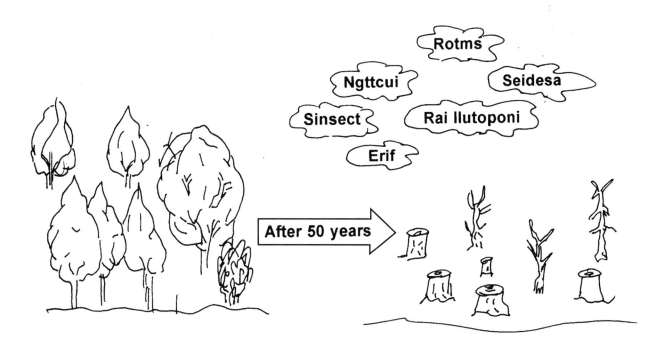

BENEFITS OF ONE TREE

Experts have attempted to put a dollar value on the benefits of trees. Let's say it costs approximately $5.00 to purchase a small tree. Assuming the tree will live and grow for 50 years, it may provide the following benefits:

BENEFITS OF ONE TREE	
Benefits That One Tree Can Provide:	**Cost to Replace with Machines or Chemicals**
Production of oxygen	$31,000
Absorbing, cleansing, and releasing water	37,000
Putting nutrients into the soil	31,000
Purifying our air by removing particulates, carbon dioxide, and other pollutants	62,000
Providing shelter and food for wildlife	31,000

INSTRUCTIONS:

Determine the total economic value of the tree.

DEFORESTATION PUZZLE

INSTRUCTIONS:

In the following table, pick out 11 words relating to forests. Words go from left to right only.

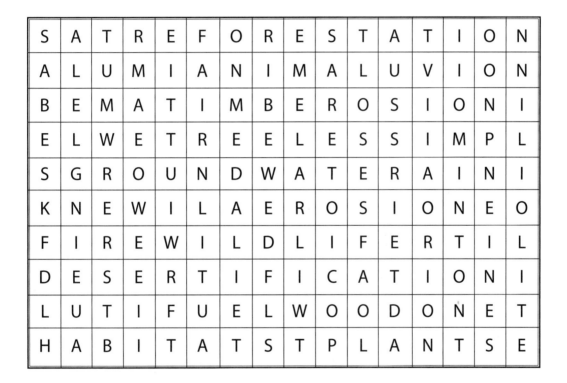

S	A	T	R	E	F	O	R	E	S	T	A	T	I	O	N
A	L	U	M	I	A	N	I	M	A	L	U	V	I	O	N
B	E	M	A	T	I	M	B	E	R	O	S	I	O	N	I
E	L	W	E	T	R	E	E	L	E	S	S	I	M	P	L
S	G	R	O	U	N	D	W	A	T	E	R	A	I	N	I
K	N	E	W	I	L	A	E	R	O	S	I	O	N	E	O
F	I	R	E	W	I	L	D	L	I	F	E	R	T	I	L
D	E	S	E	R	T	I	F	I	C	A	T	I	O	N	I
L	U	T	I	F	U	E	L	W	O	O	D	O	N	E	T
H	A	B	I	T	A	T	S	P	L	A	N	T	S	E

DEFORESTATION PUZZLE

1. REFORESTATION
2. ANIMAL
3. TIMBER
4. TREE
5. GROUNDWATER
6. EROSION
7. WILDLIFE
8. DESERTIFICATION
9. FUEL WOOD
10. PLANTS
11. HABITAT

FOREST FUNCTION AND VALUE

PRODUCTIVE

In some ways, the forest is present everywhere: at home, in the classroom, at sporting events, and in our cultural environment. If you look around, you will see many forest products—tables, chairs, furniture, toys, books, pencils, etc. Many by-products of the forest are used in the chemical industry: latex and resin, for example. Some extracts of trees and other plants are used in the pharmaceutical industry. Trees produce nuts and fruits, and we use various other forest plants and animals for food.

PROTECTIVE

Forests are like large natural houses because they provide shelter for many animals and plants. They provide efficient protection from noise, Sun, heat, wind, and some pollution. They enrich the soil through naturally composting organic matter. To some extent, forests regulate the amount and improve the quality of water within local watersheds and rivers, and they preserve humidity. Forests prevent erosion because the roots of trees hold tightly to the soil, preventing rain from washing excessive amounts of soil into rivers. In the same way, they prevent mudslides. Forests play a role in the circulation of water, carbon, nitrogen, and oxygen in nature.

CLEANING

Forests play a major role in cleaning our atmosphere by removing carbon dioxide (CO_2). Plants remove CO_2 from the air and transform it into organic matter through the process of photosynthesis. As the end result of this process, plants release oxygen into the air. Trees serve as a filter to clean air by absorbing pollutant gases and dust from the atmosphere. This filtering capacity helps to stabilize air quality, thus promoting the survival of flora and fauna that live in the forest.

CREATIVE

Often people feel the need for physical and psychic equilibrium, and many individuals achieve this equilibrium and its subsequent satisfaction in a forest environment surrounded by calm, freedom, and beauty, which is often lacking in our cities. The forest is a source of various landscapes and the color tonalities of different seasons. Many of the world's great artists have attempted to capture the beauty of the forest in photography, painting, poetry, and music.

Cultural

Throughout their existence people have had a close relationship with the forest. This is evident in mythology, religious rites, literature, and art. The reasons and the causes are to be found in the greatness and dimension of the forest and in the impressions it can leave on the mind of the individual.

Activity sheets may be downloaded from www.idebate.org/environment.htm.

FACTORS IN DEFORESTATION

HUMAN ACTIONS

+ Clearing of forests for roads, dams, or housing and for industrial development (developed countries)
+ Clearing of forests for agriculture (developing countries)
+ Over-harvesting trees
+ Over- or uncontrolled grazing
+ Acid rain and other atmospheric pollution
+ Fires

NATURAL FACTORS

+ Fires
+ Severe storms
+ Diseases
+ Harmful insects.

BIODIVERSITY—THE SPICE OF LIFE

OBJECTIVES

Upon completing this lesson, students will understand that

1. Diversity is crucial to the continued survival of life forms on the planet and

2. Diversity is natural, healthy, and necessary within all communities.

BACKGROUND

It is only recently that humans have begun to realize that biological diversity is important to the stable existence, preservation, and development of life on the planet. Scientists cannot say for certain how many species live on the Earth. They have classified approximately 1.5 million, but according to some estimates, 4–5 million remain unclassified. This diversity is vital for the survival of life on Earth. The interrelation of particular species is important for the health of ecosystems. Humans too profit from this diversity. It provides the resource base for agriculture, health, fisheries, forests, and much more. Many of the species yet to be explored may be valuable as sources of pharmaceuticals or in other areas. When human beings destroy their environment, they destroy opportunities for scientific advancement. As teachers, we must begin to stress that just as nations respect and preserve their language, traditions, and culture, they must also protect the biota in their territory.

MATERIALS

Biodiversity fact sheet (copies for each student) (optional)
Activity 1: None
Activity 2: Small pictures of organisms (a different organism for each student)
Species Biography Sheet (copies for each student)
Species Funding activity sheet (copies for each student)

TEACHER TIPS

You may want to use Biodiversity fact sheet to give your students general background on the topic.

Because human health is dependent on diversity that exists in the world around us, you may ask students to relate diversity to the philosophy of the curriculum, both discussing the flower and the concept of unity and community and how it relates to diversity.

Activity 1 is appropriate for younger students.

ACTIVITY

Activity 1: Celebrate Diversity

A selected student should write the name of an animal on a piece of paper and give this piece of paper to the teacher. Have the student stand at the front of the class. The student should say, "I am an animal that" and give clues (one at a time) to the class. Encourage students to give clues that go beyond description—habitat, use, etc. For example, the student might have selected a panda and therefore might give clues like "I am an animal that lives in China," "I am an animal that is endangered," etc. The other students may shout out the name of the animal at any time that they think they know it. The first student to guess the correct animal then goes to the front of the room, writes his or her selection on a piece of paper for the teacher, and then begins to give clues to the class.

Activity 2: Species Funding

Preparation

Ask the students to bring in small pictures of organisms. Tell them to look for a wide variety, not just mammals. Make sure the collection includes plants, animals, microorganisms, and fungi. Ask them to put the name of the organism on the back of the picture.

1. Distribute a picture to each student and ask the students to write a brief bio (description, habitat, etc.) of it, using the Species Biography Sheet.

2. Tell the class that an international wildlife federation will allocate $1 million to conservation but it needs recommendations on how to spend it. Have each student interview an "organism" and determine how much of the money should go to each. (They can decide to give no money to a species.) Have them record their recommendations on Species Funding activity sheet.

3. Create a master funding sheet of suggested spending on each organism. (The total amount will be the number of students x $1 million.) Discuss why students made their choices and how they want to spend the money. Are there any patterns? Are certain types of species neglected? Why?

SPECIES BIOGRAPHY SHEET

Name:_____

Habitat: _____

_____

_____

Place in food chain: _____

_____

_____

Status: Threatened _____Yes _____No

               Endangered _____Yes _____No

Threats to species: _____

_____

_____

Conservation measures: _____

_____

_____

_____

Possible uses:_____

_____

_____

SPECIES FUNDING

Species	$	Why?	How?

BIODIVERSITY

BACKGROUND

No one knows exactly when human beings first began to understand the concept of diversity. Perhaps it was the very first moment that a person opened his or her eyes and looked around. It is only recently, though, that we have begun to truly appreciate the value of the diversity that surrounds us.

Some time ago people began to study individual systems and to realize that individual systems operate stably because they possess inner diversity. This is true whether we are referring to an individual organism, an individual species, or an individual ecosystem. As people started to recognize the importance of inner diversity within individual systems, they also began to expand that recognition to the biosphere as a whole and to realize that biological diversity is important to the stable existence, preservation, and development of life on the planet.

As a planet, the Earth is characterized by a great diversity of natural conditions. This is caused primarily by the spherical shape of the planet, its rotation on its axis, and its rotation around the Sun. Latitudinal and seasonal changes of solar energy intensity and the Earth's varied topography provide for a diversity of ecosystems, and thus biodiversity.

A great diversity of plant, animal, fungi, and microorganism species inside ecosystems interact. Each species satisfies its basic requirements for food, energy, and information and encourages the existence of other species. Species diversity is an important condition of an ecosystem's stable operation.

One important peculiarity of every species is the variability and diversity of individuals within its population. The outward characteristics of a species are not uniformly shown with different individuals of a species, thus providing for individual diversity. The phenotype of an organism is its outward physical characteristics. This is a result of its genotype, or genetic makeup, which is inherited. Genetic variability is the basis of biodiversity and is demonstrated at all levels of life.

ECOLOGICAL DIVERSITY

An ecosystem is composed of a community of organisms that interact with each other and with their shared environment, providing stability for an unspecified amount of time. The main components of each ecosystem are biota (a collection of organisms) and abiotic factors (physical and chemical components of an environment).

The land and the ocean predetermine the existence of two basic ecosystems on our planet: land ecosystems and aquatic ecosystems. Land ecosystems include <u>tropical</u>

forests; savannas (a treeless plain or open meadow found in a tropical area, covered with thick green grass in the rainy season that withers in the dry season); chaparral (stunted forest growth found on all continents); temperate forests; prairies-steppes-pampas; deserts; boreal forests (taiga); and tundra (lowlands of the northern hemisphere on the arctic coastline, covered with snow and ice in winter and with dwarfed shrubs, lichens, and mosses in summer). Specific groups of life forms are characteristic of each of these ecosystems.

Each ecosystem's biota is represented by four kingdoms of organisms: plants, animals, microorganisms, and fungi. One of the most important trends in the relationship between people and the environment is recognition of the importance of, and the protection of, all four kingdoms. Climate is the main factor in determining what plants will exist in a community, and the plant community is the nucleus around which a particular ecosystem is created.

Water ecosystems compose the largest and most stable ecosystems, and there is great variety among them. For example, there exist seas, estuaries, seacoasts, rivers, lakes, streams, and bogs. Sea ecosystems are united in one huge ecosystem, the world ocean. Life in the ocean is affected by physical factors such as solar light intensity, temperature, salinity, currents, and tides.

Organisms are not distributed uniformly on land or at sea. There are areas of dense population and there are areas with small numbers of species and/or low population density. Areas of dense population can be observed vertically and horizontally. For example, water near the surface is the most saturated with life. Many more forms of bacteria, protozoa, mollusk larvae, worms, crustaceans, fish, and other animals are found here than in deeper layers of the ocean. Seacoasts contain more life than do areas farther from the shore.

SPECIES DIVERSITY

Scientists cannot say for certain how many species of animals, fungi, plants, and microorganisms live on the Earth. By the end of the 20th century, approximately 1.5 million species had scientific names, i.e., were considered to have been discovered and classified. According to the estimates of some scientists, 4–5 million species remained unclassified. Still other scientists think as many as 30 million species of organisms exist on the planet. One thing is certain. We are presently living in an era of maximum biotic diversity.

Scientists who study the development of life on the Earth mark five mass organism extinctions. The most famous of these is the dinosaur extinction by the end of the Mesozoic era. There was a period when life on the Earth was in danger of extinction. This was during the great Permian Catastrophe, about 240 million years ago, when 96% of sea animals became extinct. Today, because of the activities of human beings, the Earth is once again experiencing a drop in biodiversity.

Tropical rain forests are the ecosystems containing the most diversity of life forms. One explorer found 43 ant species on a single tree in a forest of Peru. Another explorer found more than 700 varieties of trees on 10 hectares of land on the island of Kalimantan in Indonesia. The two groups of living creatures that are the richest in species—arthropods, especially insects, and flowering plants—are concentrated in the tropics. Much of the tremendous diversity of tropical rain forests has yet to be explored. Many scientists feel that the cures to several human diseases may lie in these rain forests.

It is possible to classify organisms according to their contribution to the general biodiversity if one evaluates the number of species in each of the different groups. If one does this, it turns out that we are currently living in the era of insects, as they represent more than 50% of species classified by science. On the other hand, mammals and birds, taken together, represent approximately 11,000 species, which is only about 0.7% of the 1.5 million classified species.

HUMAN DIVERSITY

Although human beings are only one of the 1.5 million species that currently inhabit the planet, they are unique as biological creatures and as the possessors of ideas, culture, and spirit. Because of these factors, we have created great diversity. Human diversity differs from the diversity of other creatures in many ways. It is manifested as biological, social, cultural, and spiritual diversity. All of these help to determine an individuality for each of us. Although we have many obvious similarities, each member of the human population is a unique individual.

Therefore, human diversity is extremely vast. This species lives across the entire planet and subdivides itself into races, ethnic groups, populations, nations, and nationalities. This subdivision is based on hereditary biological characteristics as well as on social differences that are interconnected with sociocultural development. Human migration, which is currently very strong, has a great impact on the forming of new nationalities and populations.

UNIT FOUR
Getting Involved

❧

POLITICAL ACTION—WRITING LETTERS TO ACTIVATE INTEREST IN THE ENVIRONMENT

OBJECTIVES

Upon completing this lesson, students will be able to

1. Understand that each ecological problem is also a social and political problem;

2. Begin to make change by setting a positive example for others;

3. Understand that ecological problems are connected to our own behavior; and

4. Understand that we can all work, both individually and collectively, to solve specific environmental problems by writing letters.

BACKGROUND

Individuals can help the environment by changing their lifestyles—living in an environmentally friendly manner. But they can also help solve environmental problems by working through their government officials and elected representatives to effect change on a larger scale. One of the most effective ways of getting these officials interested in solving specific problems is through a letter-writing campaign. The more letters written about a particular issue, the more likely the recipient will take action. In order to be effective, these letters cannot merely express a general complaint. They must show that the writers are knowledgeable about the problem and its possible solutions. This activity takes the class through the steps necessary to gain this knowledge and to present it effectively to their representatives.

MATERIALS

Environmental Problems teacher suggestions
Environmental Problems activity sheet (copies for each student)
A Letter-Writing Campaign activity sheet (copies for each student)
Suggestions for Writing Effective Letters (copies for each student)

TEACHER TIPS

This lesson is most effective when it is reinforced a number of times so that students become comfortable in the role of political participant.

ACTIVITY

1. Distribute Environmental Problems activity sheet. Ask the students to think of specific

examples of local environmental problems and write them in the first column of the sheet. (Some possible suggestions are listed in Environmental Problems teacher suggestions.) Tell the students to think of what human behaviors contribute to the problems and note them in column two.

2. Ask the students to think of conflicts related to solving these problems and describe them in the third column. Tell them to write their suggestions for solving the problems in the fourth column.

3. After the students have completed the sheets, ask them to share their examples and compile a master list for the class.

4. Explain that the class will be conducting a letter-writing campaign asking a local official to deal with one of the problems they have listed. Tell the class to choose that item from the master list. Discuss the problem, the behaviors contributing to it, and the decisions and conflicts related to it. Encourage the class to come to some kind of consensus about the change they want made.

5. Have the class determine the best official to send the letter to.

6. Distribute A Letter-Writing Campaign activity sheet and review. Give the students several days to complete the form. Review and compile a master list.

7. Tell the students that they will now write letters to the individual asking for change. They will base their letters on their understanding of the problem and the information they gathered in completing A Letter-Writing Campaign activity sheet. You may want to distribute Suggestions for Writing Effective Letters to help them write their letters.

8. Once the students have completed their draft letters, review and return. Tell the students to make clean copies and send them to the official.

9. Monitor the official's response.

Environmental Problems

Environmental Pollution (examples)	Our Behavior That Contributes to It	Decisions and Conflicts Related to This Environmental Problem	Changes We Can Make
1. Polluted air from car exhaust and cigarette smoke	We like and need transportation. Some people are addicted to smoking.	Should we build more roads for cars, or should we invest more money in public transportation? Should we use unleaded gasoline?	
2. Food sprayed with pesticides	We don't want to buy damaged or insect-laden fruits and vegetables.	Should farmers use fewer pesticides and risk having smaller crops to sell? Should people pay more for pesticide-free food?	
3. Cutting down trees	We need paper for much of our work.	Are we willing to take the time to recycle our used school paper, office paper, and newspaper? Should we buy recycled paper even if it costs more money?	
4. Polluting air and water from power plants	We heat our homes in winter; we use electricity in our jobs and our homes.	Should we pay to insulate our homes or hot water pipes?	

Activity sheets may be downloaded from www.idebate.org/environment.htm.

ENVIRONMENTAL PROBLEMS

Local Environmental Problem	Our Behavior That Contributes to It	Decisions and Conflicts Related to This Environmental Problem	Changes We Can Make
1.			
2.			
3.			
4.			

A LETTER-WRITING CAMPAIGN

Ecological problem:_____

What we want to accomplish by writing a letter:_____
_____
_____
_____
_____

To whom we will write this letter:_____

PREPARATION QUESTIONS:

1. How can this person contribute to the solution?

2. Where does this person stand on the problem?

3. What do you think this person wants to know about the subject?

4. Will this person feel responsible for correcting the problem or will he or she think it is someone else's responsibility?

5. How do you think this person will feel about the solution you are proposing?

6. What will the solution cost the person in terms of money, time, and effort?

7. What does the environmental problem cost the community in terms of money, time, and health?

SUGGESTIONS FOR WRITING EFFECTIVE LETTERS

1. Try to be brief.

2. Be clear.

3. Demonstrate that you are well informed about all aspects of the environmental problem.

4. Support your facts with examples and evidence.

5. Always ask for a response to your letter. If you do not receive a response in a reasonable amount of time, write again.

6. Write to more than one person and inform each of the individuals of the other letters that you are writing.

7. Be respectful and tactful but determined.

8. Be patient.

9. Demonstrate that you are eager to participate actively and to assist with the solution to the problem.

MAKING A DIFFERENCE—A CAMPAIGN FOR THE ENVIRONMENT

OBJECTIVES

Upon completing this lesson, students will be able to

1. Explain the concept of change,

2. Recognize the role they can play in the process of change, and

3. Identify aspects of the environment in their community that they would like to be different.

BACKGROUND

Understanding environmental issues is very important. Without the understanding we cannot be clear about what has happened to create problems and what can be done to solve them. Beyond understanding we also need action. People need to be motivated and mobilized to bring change—to realize that one person can make a difference in creating a healthier planet. This activity can help students understand and experience how to develop a campaign for changing something related to their environment.

MATERIALS

Plan for Change activity sheet (copies for each student)

Planning a Strategy for Change resource sheet (copies for each student)

TEACHER TIPS

The amount of time needed for this activity will depend on how deeply you want the students to research their strategies for change.

ACTIVITY

1. Ask the students to discuss whether they think change is generally easy or difficult and to give the reasons for their responses. Guide the discussion so that the students at least make the following points:

   a. To change may mean to give up something. This can be easy and happy for some people and difficult and sad for others.

   b. To change means to recognize that there may be another way to accomplish something.

c. To change may mean re-thinking one's values and beliefs about how things are "sup-posed" to be.

d. To change may mean to move toward something new that may involve risks.

e. Some people may see change as a "win-lose" situation—some person or group must lose and another must win.

2. Now you can move the discussion toward environmental issues. Ask the students to brainstorm aspects of the environment in their school or community that they would like to be different. List these on the chalkboard.

3. When the brainstorming is over, ask them to decide which are the most important items on the list. (Note: the number will depend on the size of the class. Groups should not be larger than eight people.)

4. Divide the class into groups, distribute Plan for Change activity sheet, and assign each group a problem, for which they are to develop a strategy for change. Distribute and review Planning a Strategy for Change, which they can use to guide them through the process.

5. Ask each group to discuss its plan with the class. Once all groups have presented their plans, have the class set a schedule for implementing them.

PLAN FOR CHANGE

Problem:_____

_____

Goal:_____

_____

Information we need to solve the problem: _____

_____

_____

_____

What may make it easy or difficult to solve the problem? _____

_____

_____

_____

What issues may be sensitive and cause some resistance to change? Why?

_____

_____

_____

How will we overcome this resistance and these difficulties? _____

_____

_____

_____

Steps we must take to solve the problem	By whom	When
1.		
2.		
3.		
4.		

PLANNING A STRATEGY FOR CHANGE

As you plan your strategy for change, you may want to use the following questions and ideas to guide your thinking. They will help you develop a clear direction for your work.

1. What is the problem you want to solve?

2. What is the best situation that could result from your work to solve this problem?

3. What information do you need to solve the problem? How will you research it? Who do you have to talk to in order to get the information?

4. Who has to do what and when in order to solve this problem?

5. What will make it easier or more difficult to achieve your solution?

6. What can you or other people do to overcome the obstacles?

7. What are the benefits/advantages of solving this problem? Why should it be resolved?

8. How will you know you have reached your goal/been successful?

Activity sheets may be downloaded from www.idebate.org/environment.htm.

SCHOOL ENVIRONMENTAL AUDIT

OBJECTIVES

Upon completing this lesson, the students will be able to

1. Identify environmental problems in their school,

2. Evaluate different ways of solving these problems, and

3. Determine a plan of action.

BACKGROUND

In this activity students evaluate how environmentally friendly their school is. They assess problems, come up with possible solutions, and work with the school administration to make their school environmentally responsible. In the process they come to understand the realities schools face in trying to be responsible and learn that they can make a difference for the environment on the local level.

MATERIALS

School Energy Audit worksheet (copies for each member of the team)
School Waste Audit worksheet (copies for each member of the team)
Audit Task worksheet (optional)
Problem/Solution worksheet (copies for each student)

TEACHER TIPS

If the school is large, you may not be able to audit the entire building. Audit your classroom and the public areas. If possible, involve the building engineer or custodial department in the audit. Make sure to clear the audit with school administrators.

ACTIVITY

1. Tell the students that they will be conducting an environmental audit of their school, similar to the energy and waste audits they conducted at home.

2. Ask for volunteers to draw a floor plan of the school or of the area to be audited.

3. Divide the students into two teams. One will audit energy use; the other will audit waste.

4. Distribute a floor plan and School Energy Audit worksheet to each member of the energy team.

5. Distribute a floor plan and School Waste Audit worksheet to each member of the waste team.

6. Have each team decide how it will handle the audit (as a group, assigning portions to individual students, timeframe for audit, etc.). You may use Task worksheet to help them organize their audit.

7. Ask each team to report its results to the entire class.

8. Based on the audit reports, ask the class to determine five major environmental problems the school has. Write these on the board.

9. Ask the students to research how other schools have handled these problems. They may do this through letters, library or Web research, etc.

10. Distribute Problem/Solution worksheet. Divide the class into five groups and have each brainstorm possible solutions to one of the problems based on their thoughts and research. Tell them to write their possible solutions on the worksheet and evaluate each following the instructions on the form.

11. Ask each group to report its recommendations to the class.

12. Have the class draw up a report for the administration outlining the environmental problems the students found and their suggested solutions.

SCHOOL ENERGY AUDIT

GENERAL SCHOOL CONDITIONS

INSULATION AND WEATHERIZATION

Are the following insulated/weatherized?

Windows: Yes_____ No _____

Exterior Doors: Yes_____ No _____

Exterior Walls: Yes_____ No _____

Ceiling/Roof: Yes_____ No _____

LIGHTING AND EQUIPMENT

Does the school use energy efficient lighting? Yes_____ No _____

Does the school use energy-saving equipment? Yes_____ No _____

Are lights left on when not needed? Yes_____ No _____

Are computers, monitors, and other equipment left on when not being used?

Yes_____ No _____

HEATING AND COOLING

Is the system: Efficient _____ Inefficient _____

Are halls the same temperature as classrooms? Yes_____ No _____

Do people keep classroom doors closed? Yes_____ No _____

Is furniture covering heating and cooling vents? Yes_____ No _____

Are there curtains or shades to keep Sun out and heat in? Yes_____ No _____

Are there trees that act as shade or wind barriers? Yes_____ No _____

SPECIFIC PROBLEMS

Note specific problems (leaky windows, broken shades, etc.) in the table below and indicate their location on the floor plan.

Problem	Location

SCHOOL WASTE AUDIT

GENERAL SCHOOL CONDITIONS

OUR SCHOOL RECYCLES THE FOLLOWING:

Aluminum cans: Yes_____ No _____

Paper/newspaper: Yes_____ No _____

Plastic: Yes_____ No _____

Glass: Yes_____ No _____

OUR SCHOOL DONATES THE FOLLOWING:

Electronic products (computers, cell phones, etc.): _____Yes _____No

Sports equipment: _____Yes _____No

HAZARDOUS WASTE

HAZARDOUS PRODUCT USE

(hazardous products may be found in science labs and shop and art classrooms)

Name	Use	Disposal Method

SPECIFIC WASTE PROBLEMS

Note specific problems in the table below and indicate their location on the floor plan.

Problem	Location

AUDIT TASK

Task	Who Will Do It	Target Date for Completion

Activity sheets may be downloaded from www.idebate.org/environment.htm.

PROBLEM/SOLUTION

Problem: _____

INSTRUCTIONS

1. Write the proposed solution in the first column.

2. Evaluate your solution by ranking it on a scale of 0–5 under each of the three criteria. Rank the solution according to your answer to the questions in the next three columns.

3. Total the points for each solution.

4. Combine your points with those of other members of your team for each solution. Based on the numbers, which is the best solution? Do you agree with the numbers?

5. Report your group's recommendation to the class.

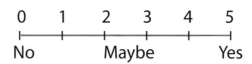

Solution	Easy to do?	Affordable?	Effective?	Total

THE CITY AS AN ECOSYSTEM

OBJECTIVES

Upon completing this lesson, students will have investigated urban ecological factors and the benefits of considering these factors during urban planning and development.

BACKGROUND

When students think of "ecosystems," they usually think of natural systems such as forests, lakes, or even gardens. They rarely think of cities. But urban environments are increasingly important ecosystems that are also threatened by human activity. This activity helps students understand the city as an ecosystem and evaluate the factors that impact that system.

MATERIALS

City as an Ecosystem activity sheet (copies for each student)

TEACHER TIPS

Make sure that students list both the positive and negative factors impacting the city. They will need this information for the next lesson, creating a future city.

ACTIVITY

1. Distribute City as an Ecosystem activity sheet. Ask the class to think of some environmental factors that can affect cities and list them on their activity sheets. These might include industrial concentration, recreational opportunities, electromagnetic fields, and traffic congestion.

2. Now ask the class to think of how these factors might have either a positive or negative effect on the city and list these effects in the appropriate column. If necessary, ask the students to research the impact of the factors they have listed.

3. Create a master table for students to use in the next lesson.

CITY AS AN ECOSYSTEM

INSTRUCTIONS:

1. Think of some environmental factors that can affect cities and list them in the first column.

2. Decide whether each factor has a positive or negative effect on the environment, or both, and check the appropriate column in the table.

3. Explain the effect of the factor in the last column.

Factor	Environmentally		Effect
	Positive	Negative	

FUTURE CITY

OBJECTIVES

Upon completing this lesson, students will

1. Consider the optimum environmental conditions for human life in a city and

2. Develop their ideal plan for ecological balance and preservation in a city.

BACKGROUND

In this lesson students will form creative teams, each of which will design a city that respects and exists in harmony with its environment. Students will also elect an Environmental Council from among their classmates that will decide which elements of each of the cities created by the student teams should be incorporated into the class-designed Future City.

MATERIALS

master City as an Ecosystem activity sheet (from previous lesson, copies for each student)
Our Future City activity sheet (copies for each student)
Future City Environmental Rules activity sheet (copies for each student)
Construction paper in various colors
Large piece of cardboard for each group and one for the class design of Future City
Tape
Glue
Markers

TEACHER TIPS

Instead of building a three-dimensional city, the students may want to draw a map of their city, indicating the placement of various buildings, parks, etc.

When your class has finished deciding on the environmental rules that will govern Future City, the students might like to determine whether or not any of these rules are in place in their city. If they are not, have your class decide on various methods that they could use to present their ideas to city planners and to other city officials. It might be possible to incorporate some of these ideas into the city or neighborhood in which they live.

ACTIVITY

1. Divide the class into groups. Each group should be given one of the large pieces of cardboard. They will use this as the foundation on which to build their three-dimensional, environmentally friendly city. You may set up specific geographic features for the city. For example, you might decide that there is a river running through the center of the city; that there is a large lake located on the northwestern edge; that there are mountains on the eastern edge, etc. All student teams would then have to incorporate these features into their design. Remember to tell them that this is to be a large city with industry.

2. Tell the students to build their cities taking into consideration the environmental factors they listed in the City as an Ecosystem master sheet from the previous lesson. Tell your students that, as they are designing their city, they should consider the quality of life for the residents of their community. They should make decisions regarding many environmental questions such as the following:

   + Will there be trees, shrubs, flowers, and vegetable gardens in your city? Where will they be planted? Who will plant and care for them? What varieties will be planted? Why are these specific varieties being chosen?

   + Where is the drinking water source located and how is its quality protected?

   + How will your city handle its solid waste problems?

   + What types of industry are located in your city and where are they allowed to locate?

   + What types of transportation are available? Are some types of transportation environmentally preferable to others?

3. As the teams are building their city, they should note details regarding the decisions they are making and why they are making them on Our Future City activity sheet. For example, if they are creating a park in the center of the city, they should explain why they put it there—perhaps so that office workers will have a quiet place to go during lunchtime. They should be prepared to discuss their decisions and the reasoning behind them when each group describes its city to the rest of the class.

4. Suggest to your students that, when designing their city, they can consider any factors that are important to them. They may decide to include many additional details in the design and description of their city such as trade, sports, tourism, culture, education, medical establishments, police and fire protection, etc.

5. After the groups have completed their cities, have the students elect an Environmental Council. They should consider who among them has researched specific pollution problems or demonstrated knowledge of these problems during the previous lessons and during the construction of their cities.

6. After the election, ask your Environmental Council members to sit together near the front of the room. Have each student team display and explain its city. Each team should choose one of its members to make the initial presentation. That person should refer to the written comments when necessary. Allow the other team members to make additional comments and have a question and answer session involving the entire class following each team's presentation.

7. After the presentations have been completed, bring the remaining piece of cardboard to the front of the room and explain to your class that now the Environmental Council will choose the best environmental components of the various cities and incorporate them into a Future City. The Environmental Council members should explain the reasons for their decisions to the rest of the class. If there are disagreements among the Environmental Council members, they should vote on which elements to move to Future City. As the Environmental Council makes its decisions, members of the student teams remove those elements from their cities and establish them in Future City.

   If none of the cities designed by the student teams has addressed a critical area, such as solid waste, ask the class to address and design the element for Future City.

8. After the class has built Future City, have the students decide on the environmental rules that govern it. For example:

   - Do the residents of Future City utilize water and electric power economically? How does the city government encourage this?

   - What are the rules that govern use of parks and public gardens?

   - Are there restrictions concerning fire safety?

   - Is your city making an effort to preserve and enlarge green zones?

   - Does your city make an effort to feed birds and/or other animals in the winter time?

   - Is there a noise ordinance in place in specific areas of the city?

   - Are there a sufficient number of solid waste receptacles located in various areas of the city?

   Tell the students to return to their original groups and develop these rules. Distribute Future City Environmental Rules activity sheet and tell the teams to write their rules and their reasons for suggesting each rule on the sheet.

9. Ask each group to present its rules to the class. Have the students vote on adopting the rule, and if it is adopted, write it on a master list that the class can present with its Future City.

OUR FUTURE CITY

Elements We are Including in Our City	Why
1.	
2.	
3.	
4.	
5.	
6.	
7.	
8.	
9.	
10.	

FUTURE CITY ENVIRONMENTAL RULES

Environmental Rules Governing Our City	Why We Suggest the Rule
1.	
2.	
3.	
4.	
5.	
6.	
7.	
8.	
9.	
10.	

Activity sheets may be downloaded from www.idebate.org/environment.htm.

BRINGING EARTH DAY TO YOUR COMMUNITY

OBJECTIVES

Upon completing this lesson, students will be able to

1. List the reasons why people and the environment are interdependent;

2. Feel appreciation, love, and responsibility to care for the environment;

3. Plan Earth Day activities; and

4. Involve their parents and the community in their Earth Day activities.

BACKGROUND

Middle school students are beginning to make conscious and independent decisions. They are eager to learn and to develop their independent personalities. If they understand the links between their behavior and the environment, young people will act responsibly. Therefore, they need to be taught how they can improve the environment through their behavior, and how to conduct activities that will help to raise the awareness of their parents, neighbors, friends, and the entire community concerning the need to protect the environment. April 22, Earth Day, is an ideal time to conduct positive environmental actions that reach out into the surrounding community and help students understand the serious environmental problems facing the Earth.

MATERIALS

April 22—Earth Day information sheet (copies for each student)
Activity 1: Most Serious Environmental Problem activity sheet (copies for each student)
Research Questions activity sheet (multiple copies for each student)
Activity 2: Earth Day Activities resource sheet
Earth Day Celebration Task Sheet (copies for each student)

TEACHER TIPS

We have developed this material to be used throughout the month of April in which Earth Day takes place. Begin discussing Earth Day early in the month so that your have ample time to plan and implement activities.

ACTIVITY

Distribute April 22—Earth Day information sheet and discuss the significance of Earth Day.

Activity 1: Environmental Grants

1. Ask the students to list the most serious environmental problems facing the Earth.

2. Divide the class into small groups (no more than five students) and assign a problem to each group. Tell them that an international philanthropic organization has announced a grant of $10 million to the group that can show its problem is most serious and that can suggest the best ways of dealing with the problem. Each group will have to submit a "grant proposal" (a written report) and make a five-minute oral presentation to justify their case.

3. Tell the groups that they must research their issue. Distribute Most Serious Environmental Problem activity sheet and ask them to work together to determine what research questions they have to answer and which members of the group will answer them. Tell them to use Research Questions answer sheet to record their information.

4. Once the groups have finished their research, ask them to develop an outline for their grant proposal. Remind them that the outline must have two main sections—the first outlining the problem and the second discussing their solution—and that each section should be as detailed as possible.

5. When the groups are satisfied with their outlines, collect and review them, making suggestions that will help strengthen the presentations.

6. Return the outlines to the groups and tell the students to begin writing their grant proposal. They may do this as a group or they may elect an individual to write the initial draft and then edit the student's proposal. Encourage them to include artwork to illustrate their main points.

7. Collect and review the grants, making suggestions for improvement. Return to the students and ask them to polish their proposals.

8. Ask each group to choose one member who will present the proposal. Have each group develop the presentation and rehearse it with their spokesperson. Remind them that they have no more than five minutes to speak.

9. After the presentations are completed, the class can vote on who will get the money. Or you can announce that the organization was so impressed with the presentations that all the groups will receive a grant!

Activity 2: Planning Local Earth Day Activities

1. Ask the students to suggest activities for Earth Day that will benefit their school or neighborhood and involve their parents and the community. Write these on the chalkboard. (You may want to consult Earth Day Activities resource sheet.)

2. Tell the students to vote on which activity they would like to sponsor.

3. Once the class has decided on the activities, tell the students that they will have to plan the events carefully and ask them to brainstorm the steps needed to plan a successful event. Distribute Earth Day Celebration Tasks Sheet and determine who will complete the tasks. Students may work individually or in groups.

4. Before the students begin working on their tasks, also schedule periodic progress meetings to make sure all tasks are completed on schedule.

5. On April 22 implement the activity.

APRIL 22—EARTH DAY

Earth Day, April 22, is the day when, at least once in 365 days, the attention of people all over the world is focused on the environment. Individuals, groups, and movements join on that day in their common concern for the Earth. The public concentrates on the ways that human behavior is affecting our shared environment. People become aware of the need to protect the planet by altering their own actions.

Earth Day began on April 22, 1970, when American senator Gaylord Nelson founded the first Earth Day in an effort to call public attention to the need for laws to clean up polluted rivers and other sources of drinking water. Behind the scenes, environmental activist Dennis Hayes attracted public attention to problems that had appeared and were threatening the environment. In the years that followed, Earth Day became an annual event in the United States. Students, environmentalists, and many other people interested in protecting the environment engaged in various programs and activities to publicize environmental concerns and to clean up their local environment.

In 1990 Earth Day became a global event. Millions of people all over the world participated in various activities and thus helped to raise awareness of the need to protect the environment. Since 1990 the non-profit organization Earth Day International has been active coordinating the Earth Day activities of over 3,200 organizations in 141 countries.

Activity sheets may be downloaded from www.idebate.org/environment.htm.

MOST SERIOUS ENVIRONMENTAL PROBLEM

RESEARCH QUESTIONS WE MUST ANSWER	
Question	**Who Will Research**
1.	
2.	
3.	
4.	
5.	
6.	
7.	
8.	
9.	
10.	

RESEARCH QUESTIONS

Question:_____

_____

Answer:_____

_____

_____

_____

_____

_____

_____

_____

_____

_____

Source: _____

Author:_____

Title:_____

_____

Publisher:_____

Date of publication:_____

Pages cited:_____

URL:_____

Activity sheets may be downloaded from www.idebate.org/environment.htm.

EARTH DAY ACTIVITIES

Over the past years several types of activities have become very common ways of recognizing Earth Day in America. Your students might be interested in incorporating some of these ideas into their own Earth Day plans. Examples include the following:

+ Essay and/or poster contests

+ Tree-planting ceremonies

+ Lectures and slide shows

+ Creating and giving environmental awards (to local individuals who have done positive things for the environment over the past year, or to local businesses that have implemented ecologically sensitive business practices)

+ Building and mounting birdhouses and nesting boxes for target species

+ Environmental parades

+ Environmental fairs (where business people can display the environmentally sensitive things that they manufacture and sell, and/or environmental government agencies and environmental non-governmental organizations can have displays showing the environmental work that they are involved in)

+ Adopting local streams

+ Cleaning vacant lots (and developing them into gardening areas or natural areas)

+ Creating and/or maintaining nature trails for hiking or bicycling

+ Creating environmental public service announcements for radio or writing articles or letters to newspaper editors on environmental topics

EARTH DAY CELEBRATION

Earth Day Activity:_____

Organizing an activity requires the timely completion of many tasks such as

- Writing letters notifying:

    parents

    local authorities

    local media

    local environmental organizations

- Generating Publicity:

    creating posters

    creating flyers to post (with permission) in the school halls, local churches, stores, etc.

- Finding sponsors to cover the cost of supplies and perhaps refreshments

- Collecting and organizing materials and equipment

The tasks involve you, but they can also involve your parents and teachers.

Make lists of tasks that the class needs to accomplish and assign someone to complete each task. Be sure to include dates by which tasks should be completed.

TASKS TO BE COMPLETED

PUBLICITY		
Task	**By Whom**	**By When**
1.		
2.		
3.		
4.		
5.		

LETTER WRITING		
Task	**By Whom**	**By When**
1.		
2.		
3.		
4.		
5.		

SPONSORS		
Task	**By Whom**	**By When**
1.		
2.		
3.		
4.		
5.		

MATERIALS		
Task	**By Whom**	**By When**
1.		
2.		
3.		
4.		
5.		

OTHER STUDENT TASKS		
Task	**By Whom**	**By When**
1.		
2.		
3.		
4.		
5.		

TEACHER TASKS		
Task	**By Whom**	**By When**
1.		
2.		
3.		
4.		
5.		

PARENT TASKS		
Task	**By Whom**	**By When**
1.		
2.		
3.		
4.		
5.		

WHAT CAN YOU DO?

OBJECTIVES

Upon completing this lesson, students will be able to list at least five things they can do to clean up their environment.

BACKGROUND

It is important for students to focus continually on their own involvement with environmental issues and their own connection to the Earth. This activity reinforces the philosophy of the curriculum—the need to unify our efforts to work toward a healthy environment.

MATERIALS

Environment Project activity sheet (copies for each student)
Resources depend on students' topic selection

TEACHER TIPS

You can use this lesson at any time and repeat it often. Students can make class projects, school projects, and community projects. The more involved students become, the more apt they are to begin working on environmental issues.

ACTIVITY

1. Begin the activity with an overview of the curriculum philosophy. Explain that we must continually work toward making positive change. Each student individually can make a difference. And if we all work together, we really can make positive change in our world.

2. Ask the students to find a partner. Each team is to create a project that can improve the environment. Offer them suggestions such as

   + Start an environment club

   + Search for groups within their community that they can join

   + Collect newspaper articles concerning the environment and respond to them

   + Write to a government official concerning an environmental issue that faces their community

   + Write to a company that is doing something to the Earth that is harmful

- Make posters and flyers concerning an environmental issue and distribute them for public awareness

This activity allows students the freedom to design their own "Save the Earth" projects.

3. Have the students develop their plan of action. They can start by filling in the Environment Project activity sheet.

4. Review these objectives with your students. The objectives must be clear and reasonable. Students must be able to accomplish the task within the time period allotted.

5. Ask the teams to share their projects with the class. If teams have similar goals, they may work together to accomplish them.

6. Schedule reviews of the plans: in two days, in a week, in a month.

ENVIRONMENTAL PROJECT

PROJECT	
What my team wants to accomplish	**What we need to do to reach our goals**
1. In the next 2 days:	1.
	2.
	3.
2. By next week:	1.
	2.
	3.
3. By next month:	1.
	2.
	3.

Join in, Mother and Father—We Need Your Help Too!

OBJECTIVES

Upon completing this lesson, students will be able to organize a Parents' Night, informing their parents of the environmental issues they are studying.

BACKGROUND

Change occurs only when all parts of the community work together. Students cannot successfully achieve environmental change unless they work together with other important persons in their community, including their parents. It is essential that parents learn to understand their children's interests and needs to help them achieve their goals. Working together can help the environment and will strengthen the bond between children and parents.

MATERIALS

Parent Questionnaire activity sheet (copies for each student)
Parents' Night planning sheet (copies for each student)
or
Environmental Brochure resource sheet (copies for each student)
Resources vary depending on the topic

TEACHER TIPS

This activity can be as sophisticated and complex as the teacher and school permit.

ACTIVITY

1. Discuss the need to have parents work with children for environmental change.

2. Distribute copies of Parent Questionnaire activity sheet and tell the students to ask their parents to fill it out. Reword the questionnaire to add any other issues the students would like to discuss with their parents.

3. Once the questionnaires are complete, compile a master questionnaire to see which issue is of most interest to parents. Develop an information night centered around that topic or work with the students to create a brochure on the topic that they can take home.

4. If you do have a Parents' Night, use Parents' Night planning sheet to help organize the activity. If the students want to develop a brochure, use Environmental Brochure resource sheet to help them plan.

PARENT QUESTIONNAIRE

The most important change that needs to be made in the environment is the following:_____

_____

_____

_____

I would like to know more about the following environmental issues (check as many as needed):

____ Deforestation and how it affects my life

____ Laws and the environment

____ Water and air pollution

____ How streams, lakes, and other bodies of water affect our lives

____ Pesticides and food

____ What lead poisoning has to do with my child

____ How endangered species affect me and my family

____ What industrial pollution surrounds me—and what I can do about it

____ Where our water comes from and how it is made safe

____ Illnesses related to environmental pollution

Other:_____

I would be most interested in learning about these things ____from a brochure

____during a Parent's Night ____both.

PARENTS' NIGHT

Hosting a Parents' Night requires careful planning. Below are some of the things you have to think about.

From whom in the school administration do we need permission to hold the event?

What concerns might that person have and how will we address them?

How will we inform our parents about the event?

Flyers

Letters

Other

How are we going to present the environmental issue?

Posters

Environmental Displays

Experiments

Individual or group presentations

Other

How will we make our parents feel welcome?

Provide healthy snacks

Provide badges so everyone will know each other's names

Conduct ice-breaking activities or games that will bring parents and students together

Other

Activity sheets may be downloaded from www.idebate.org/environment.htm.

ENVIRONMENTAL BROCHURE

Below are the steps you will need to take in developing your brochure:

1. Create an outline of your topic.

2. Determine how long (how many pages) you want your brochure to be.

3. Research the elements of your outline.

4. Write the draft text of your brochure.

5. Compile or draw the artwork for your brochure.

6. Edit the draft text to make sure you have covered all themes in your outline in a logical manner.

7. Check your text for spelling and grammar.

8. Layout the brochure, putting text and artwork in place.

9. Proofread your brochure to correct any final errors.

10. Create a cover and cover art.

11. Assemble the brochure and duplicate.

Activity sheets may be downloaded from www.idebate.org/environment.htm.

GLOBAL ENVIRONMENTAL CONTEST

OBJECTIVES

Upon completing this lesson, students will be able to move beyond the limitations of this curriculum in their pursuit of environmental knowledge.

BACKGROUND

As you already know, the lessons in this curriculum are designed to help students to develop appreciation, concern, and love for the Earth and to see themselves as members of a global community charged with its protection. If we have been successful, the students' desire to gain the knowledge necessary to complete this task of protecting the Earth will naturally follow. This contest, similar to a spelling or geography bee, encourages students to study environmental issues in depth.

MATERIALS

Global Environmental Contest planning sheet
Tables
Chairs
Signs for each topic area
Multiple copies of topic area tests

TEACHER TIPS

You may want to consult Global Environmental Contest planning sheet, which outlines the steps and personnel needed in setting up the contest.

This activity can be as sophisticated and complex as you want and the school permits. You can conduct it as a class or in conjunction with other classes or other schools.

Not every station has to test the student teams. You might want to include some "just for fun" stations that allow students to rest and enjoy themselves between testing locations.

PREPARATION

You will need to engage the help of parents and environmental professionals well in advance to conduct this activity. A few days before the contest, you will have to duplicate all testing materials. You will also need to determine the position of all testing stations and draw the map students will use during the competition.

ACTIVITY

A. BACKGROUND

1. Solicit the involvement of professionals from various environmental areas for help in your contest. Your response will determine the topic areas covered in the competition. If you choose not to use professionals, determine the range of environmental topics you want covered.

2. Announce the topic areas covered in the contest.

3. Ask the students who will be participating in the contest to form teams of up to five students, or assign students to each team. Allow each team to select its own team name.

4. Each team should have an adult to serve as an adviser. One adult can serve more than one team.

5. Adult advisers and student teams should determine times for study and the methods employed for their study.

B. PREPARATION:

1. Work with the environmental professionals to develop a series of questions for each environmental area in the contest. These may include the identification of organisms or specimens, which they will have to bring with them on the day of the contest. Alternately, develop the tests yourself and provide answer sheets for the parents who will be in charge of each station.

2. Lay out the competition setting, assigning each topic area a specific station. Ideally, you will want to hold the contest outside to utilize the natural environment.

3. Prepare maps of the testing area that include the location of each testing station and the path to be followed from station to station. Duplicate copies for all participants and copies of all testing materials for each team.

4. Determine the time permitted at each station and decide on a mechanism for indicating to team members when it is time to move from one station to another. A loud buzzer or bell that can be heard across the entire contest area is ideal.

5. On the day of the contest ask the parents and professionals to arrive at the area before the student teams to set up their materials.

6. After the student teams arrive, register each team and supply the team names to the individuals in charge at each contest station. Give all participants maps of the testing area.

7. Assign each team a station at which to begin the contest. (If there are a large number of teams, you may have more than one team at a station, but try to limit the number.) This assignment and the fact that the teams must follow the path indicated on the map in moving from station to station will insure an orderly progression of students through the contest.

C. THE ENVIRONMENTAL CONTEST

1. Before the contest begins, explain that each team is to walk to its first assigned testing area. Once there they are to wait for the sound of the beginning bell. At the sound of the

bell, the individuals in charge of the testing stations will pass out one copy of the test to each team present. The team will write its team name at the top of the page and work together to complete the questions. When student teams have finished at each station, they will hand their test back to the individual in charge and will wait for the sound of the bell. At the sound of the bell, students should run to the next station following the predetermined path. (The reason for running is that the time utilized for traveling from station to station is included in the timing of the test. Of course, running also adds to the fun and excitement!) If a team has not completed a test at the sound of the bell, it must hand the test in anyway and move on to the next station.

2. An adult at each station should determine the number of correct answers on each team answer sheet immediately after the team moves on to the next station. The adult should mark the number of correct answers (points) clearly on the top of each answer sheet and submit the sheet to the test coordinator, who will keep the master list of teams and points. These results should be kept secret until the end of the contest

3. After all student teams have completed the contest and results are tabulated, assemble the teams and announce the first-, second-, and third-place winners.

4. While final results are being tabulated, you may want to offer lunch or a snack to all participants. You might also want to present an enjoyable environmental program.

5. After announcing the contest winners, award their prizes. Perhaps you and your school can locate businesses that are able to donate prizes or that will lend financial support to purchase prizes. T-shirts, which have been printed with the title and year of the environmental contest, are among the most appreciated prizes. You might even decide to have another contest earlier in the year to design the logo for the prize-winning T-shirts!

GLOBAL ENVIRONMENTAL CONTEST

CONTEST PERSONNEL

You will need the following (and maybe more) to help run your contest:

+ Team advisers

+ Environmental professionals or adults for each test station

+ Registration coordinator

+ Setup and cleanup crew

+ Food crew (if serving refreshments)

+ Test coordinator (to record test scores)

+ Test collector (to collect tests from stations)

+ Janitor

CONTEST PLANNING TIMETABLE

A few months before the contest

- Pick a date for your contest.
- Enlist the help of the environmental professionals or parents you will need for your contest.
- Determine the topic areas the contest will cover.
- Organize teams and coordinate advisers and study times.
- Determine the space you will need for the contest and complete the paperwork to reserve it if necessary.
- Determine materials (tables, chairs, etc.) you will need.
- Conduct fund-raisers or identify sponsors that might help fund contest expenses, such as refreshments and trophies.

At least one month before the contest

- If you are having refreshments, identify the supplier and order the food.
- Remind the environmental professionals participating of the date by which they have to have their test materials to you (at least two weeks before the contest).
- Order prizes.

One to two weeks before the contest

- Hold an orientation session for the adults involved in the contest or send them written instructions detailing the time and place of the contest as well as the contest rules.

- Plan the layout of the contest area and draw a map of the setting and the path the teams will follow.
- Duplicate all contest materials.
- Prepare signs for each station.
- Check on prizes.

Day before the Contest:

- Set up tables and chairs and post signs.
- Check on the refreshments.

Day of the Contest

- Set out refreshments.
- Before the contest begins, have a brief meeting with the adults to ensure that they are on the same page. Explain the following:

    - The layout of the contest area and the path of the teams
    - Distribution of tests
    - Time limits at each station
    - Instructions for returning the tests to the test coordinator

- Set up coordinator who will record team points.
- Enlist a volunteer to collect the tests quickly and return them to the contest coordinator.
- Explain the contest rules to the teams:

    - Contest path
    - Team members work together to answer questions
    - Time limits at each station

- Set up awards ceremony.

Remember to be environmentally responsible and clean up the area!

APPENDIXES

☙

ICEBREAKERS

1: ENVIRONMENTAL BINGO

1. Distribute copies of Environmental Bingo to each student.

2. Give the students 20 minutes to circulate around the room. Have each student sign a square that describes himself or herself. Each student is to sign only one square on each sheet.

3. The activity ends when one person has completed five blocks in a row horizontally, vertically, or diagonally. (Some squares may have no names if no one fits the description in these boxes.)

BELIEVES IN POSITIVE THINKING	HAS HOPE FOR THE FUTURE OF OUR PLANET	BELIEVES THAT WE WASTE TOO MUCH PAPER	IS WILLING TO HELP DEVELOP A PLAN TO CLEAN OUR PLANET	HAS A BROTHER
LOVES SCHOOL	HAS BROWN EYES	DOES NOT LITTER	LISTENS TO MUSIC QUIETLY	WALKS OR TAKES MASS TRANSIT TO SCHOOL
HAS A GOOD SENSE OF HUMOR	IS WEARING BLUE	BELIEVES THAT EACH OF US MUST HELP TO HAVE CLEAN AIR	BELIEVES THAT POLLUTION IS BAD FOR ALL OF US	HAS LIVED IN ANOTHER CITY
TURNS OFF THE LIGHTS IN HIS/HER HOME	LIKES THIS ACTIVITY	TURNS OFF THE WATER WHEN BRUSHING HIS/HER TEETH	LIKES TO VOLUNTEER AND ASSIST IN AFTER SCHOOL PROJECTS	IS AN ONLY CHILD
HAS A LOT OF ENERGY	IS A GOOD STUDENT IN SCIENCE	IS WILLING TO MAKE CHANGES TO HELP THE ENVIRONMENT	IS HAPPY TO LEARN ABOUT OUR ENVIRONMENT	RECYCLES

ICEBREAKERS

2: STUDENT PHILOSOPHIES AND RESPONSES

1. Ask each student to write one sentence, slogan, or phrase that describes the student's philosophy on environmental education.

2. Ask the students to pair off. Tell them to exchange papers, read one another's philosophies, and respond non-verbally to what each has written. For example, they may smile, nod in agreement, grimace, raise their eyebrows in surprise, etc.

3. After this exchange, each student takes back her paper and repeats the process with a new partner until she has shown her slogan to all members of the class.

4. Ask the students to share their feelings, thoughts, and impressions.

ICEBREAKERS

3: ALL ABOUT YOU

This activity provides students the opportunity to get to know one another's thoughts concerning environmental issues, and to perform various physical actions as a unified group.

1. Make the following statements and ask the students to respond.

    a. If you believe it is necessary to conserve water, clap your hands.

    b. If you turn off the water when brushing your teeth, jump up and down.

    c. If you believe smoking is harmful, stamp your feet.

    d. If your parents smoke, blink your eyes.

    e. If you don't like the smell of pollution, fan in front of your face.

    f. If you do not litter, stand up.

    g. If you turn off the lights when you leave a room, close your eyes.

    h. If you are careful with the paper you use, and don't waste it, blink your eyes.

    i. If you think it is good to save the environment, stamp your feet.

    j. If you would like to start a recycling program in our school, rub your hands.

2. Ask the participants, "What did you learn about the others that you didn't know before?" "What did you learn from this activity?" "What did you learn about yourself?"

ICEBREAKERS

4: MY THOUGHTS

This icebreaker helps the students get acquainted with others by sharing their thoughts about certain environmental issues.

1. Ask the students to complete My Thoughts activity sheet.
2. When the students have finished, re-read each statement and ask the students to share their responses with the class.

MY THOUGHTS

a. The most important change that needs to be made in the environment is

_____

b. I believe that by the year 2030 our planet will be

_____

c. When my parents ask me to turn off the lights and conserve energy, I

_____

d. If my best friend littered the street, I would

_____

e. I believe that it is important to study about the environment because

_____

f. I believe that I can help our planet by

_____

g. When people ask me if I mind if they smoke, I tell them

_____

h. The main reason I want a healthy environment is

_____

i. I believe that it is my responsibility to help our environment by

_____

j. I think I can assist our community in a cleanup by

_____

k. When I think of problems in our environment, the most dangerous one is

_____

ICEBREAKERS

5: MY WORLD/OUR WORLD

This activity allows students to understand their vision for the future.

1. Explain to the students that this activity will allow them to focus on their own life and their world.

2. Distribute copies of My World/Our World activity sheet. Ask students to draw a picture or write a short description in each of the boxes that shows an event that was or will be important to them. When they draw the picture of our world 100 years from now, ask them to draw something that will signify their outlook on the future.

3. Divide the participants into groups of four or five and have them share their life events—past, present, and future with one another.

MY WORLD/OUR WORLD

My life 5 years ago	My life now

My life in 10 years	Our world in 100 years

Activity sheets may be downloaded from www.idebate.org/environment.htm.

ICEBREAKERS

6: UNITY– COMMUNITY

1. Tell the students that they are going to work together. Divide the class into two teams (if there is an uneven number, one student may compete twice).

2. Ask the students to line up in two even lines and face the blackboard. Give the first person in each team's line a piece of chalk.

3. Explain that each team member is responsible for writing a complete sentence on a topic you have chosen (see below). The first person in each team begins by writing one word. He or she then gives the chalk to the second team member and so on. The last person completes the sentence. The final result must be a complete sentence. Students are not allowed to talk with one another. The team that completes a sentence first is the winner.

Designate one of the following topics:

Saving the Earth

Acid Rain

Air Pollution

Unifying Our School to Improve Our Environment

APPENDIX 2
WORKING WITH PARENTS

Parents need information about environmental concerns. They should be informed about the lessons that are being taught in the school. This is especially important because the philosophy of this environmental curriculum emphasizes the themes of unity and community. Parents play a major role in this unification. We believe that uniting our schools, families, and communities will provide a strong link that will help bring about environmental change. Parents must be informed of this philosophy. They need to know that their children are involved in a curriculum that is working toward making the world a better, healthier place. Parents may need encouragement to become involved. Most parents are extremely busy with jobs, household responsibilities, and their children's activities. Sometimes they are too tired to attend a program at school. It is very important, though, that the teacher use various methods to involve parents in this environmental education. Only through unifying our efforts will change occur.

Students between the ages of 10 and 14 may begin to become more independent. They may not want their parents to be as involved as when they were younger. Through activities that are age appropriate, parents can become involved without pressuring the child. Examples of activities in this curriculum that can include parents are the following:

+ bringing Earth Day into the community

+ a Parents' Night to discuss topics pertinent to your own community, such as deforestation, recycling, and air pollution

+ writing letters to activate interest in the environment

Children at this age need their parents to be involved in their lives. Schools should consider the following in working with parents:

+ Parents should be informed about the entire environmental program being offered in the school.

+ Parents need information about the environmental issues that are discussed in the classroom.

+ Parents must be encouraged to keep an open line of communication with the school, so that any questions they have about what is being taught can be handled effectively and in a timely fashion.

Schools might involve parents in the following ways:

+ Conduct educational sessions for parents to provide them with information and skills.

+ Develop homework assignments that involve students in conversation with people in their family.

+ Send parents a newsletter written by their child's class about issues that concern their children.

+ Send parents pamphlets, flyers, and updates on environmental issues.

+ Inform parents about the resources in the community that might provide them with information and opportunities for discussion. Work with leaders in the community who might be interested in developing a partnership to provide education for parents.

+ Plan educational programs for students and their parents together, so they can share information and keep open lines of communication in the family.

+ Invite parents to visit their children's classrooms and participate in activities concerning the environment.

WORKING WITH THE COMMUNITY

Beyond school-based and family efforts, the community as a whole has an important place in environmental education. To develop programs that reach into the community, the school must bring together not only experts on environmental topics but also the local people who are involved with environmental issues. A community project needs planning. Whether planning is simple or elaborate, the process generally includes the following steps:

- needs assessment
- development of long-term goals
- development of short-term goals
- development of a plan of action
- identification of resources
- identification of funding sources when applicable
- assignment of leadership tasks
- implementation
- evaluation
- program revision based on evaluation findings

Following is an example of a simple plan to organize involvement in the community.

PLANNING STEPS FOR ORGANIZING A BASIC ENVIRONMENTAL ISSUE PROJECT	
Needs Assessment	What environment problems does our community need to address?
Development of Long-term Goals	What do environmental activists want to achieve during the community project?
Development of Short-term Goals	What results can be achieved in the near future?
Development of Plan of Action	What steps can be taken to achieve short-term and long-term goals?
Identification of Resources	What resources do the school and community need to achieve the objectives?

Identification of Funding Source	Where will the money come from to organize this program?
Assignment of Leadership Tasks	Who is responsible for each part of this environmental program?
Implementation	What procedures will keep the program directed toward its goals?
Evaluation	How can the school and community determine whether the objectives are met?
Program Revision	What changes are needed to improve the community program?

There are many types of community involvement. A plan such as the one suggested is for intense involvement of school, family, and community. Other suggestions for community involvement include the following:

+ Encourage local newspapers to run articles about environmental concerns that might be important to families and the community.

+ Begin an environmental page in the newspaper to which people can write letters with questions and information about the environment.

+ Encourage local groups, including religious groups, organizations, and businesses to conduct programs about the environment.

+ Encourage local libraries to highlight books that deal with the environment.

+ Encourage local health care providers to become involved as advisers to your programs and to those in the community.

+ Develop environmental clubs. Hold community forums.

+ Develop school-business partnerships to work on environmental issues.

+ Develop through the school a library of environmental materials for community members.

+ Develop Parent Peer Groups. Organize Parent-Training Seminars.

+ Have students initiate Youth-to-Youth Team Training.

+ Utilize retirees in environmental projects.

APPENDIX 4
SMALL-GROUP INSTRUCTION

Use the following guidelines to help maximize the learning potential of small groups:

1. The ideal size for a small group is from five to seven students.

2. When forming small groups for the first time, devote time to having students learn about one another. A few moments devoted to interpersonal exchange can substantially improve the learning climate.

3. Identify student resources and use them. Students' interests and hobbies make them valuable resources for class sessions. They can bring their experiences to the classroom to illustrate concepts or to use as starting points for discussions.

4. Identify potential student leadership skills and use them whenever possible. Have students help you by running small groups and suggesting activities for class.

DIVIDING STUDENTS INTO GROUPS OR PAIRS

Many activities in this curriculum require the class to be divided into small groups. Students frequently feel anxious when asked to select a partner or join a group. To divide students in a way in which they will feel comfortable, we suggest "counting off." For example, if you have 30 students in your class and you want to divide them into six small groups, ask the students to count off beginning with the number one and ending with five and then back to one again until all of the students have a number. After the students have counted off, ask each "number" to form a group.

You can use the count-off method to pair off students or you can

1. Instruct students to raise either arm and find someone with the same arm raised,

2. Have students find someone wearing the same color,

3. Tell students to write down the number one or two on a piece of paper and find someone with the other number, or

4. Randomly divide the students.

Date Due

NOV 2 0 2006			